TRUSTED WITH THE TASK

A BIBLICAL GUIDE FOR CHURCH TRUSTEES

PASTOR STEVEN PRATT, JR.

Copyright © 2025 by Canada Church Planting
All Scripture quotations are taken from the King James Version (KJV).

All rights reserved. No part of this book may be reproduced, stored in a retrieval system, or transmitted in any form or by any means, electronic, mechanical, photocopy, recording, or otherwise, without the written permission of the publisher, except for brief quotations in printed reviews.

To contact us or order:
email@canadachurchplanting.com
http://www.canadachurchplanting.com

Dedication

To all the trustees of

FaithWay Bible Baptist Church Calgary

May God bless you abundantly as you serve Him and His church with humility, wisdom, and faithfulness.

Acknowledgments

First and foremost, I want to thank my incredible wife, **Laura**, and our daughter, **Elizabeth**, for the countless hours of sacrifice, grace, and patience that made this book possible. Laura, your unwavering support, late-night conversations, and steady encouragement were a source of strength at every step. Elizabeth, thank you for understanding when Daddy needed time to write. Your joy and love kept me going more than you'll ever know.

To **Ligaya Pinga**, our faithful church secretary, thank you for all the after-hours work, including all the detailed proofreading, as well as your willingness to serve behind the scenes and your heart for the ministry. Your diligence and care helped bring clarity and polish to every page of this book.

To those who serve faithfully alongside me in ministry, your example of humility, faithfulness, and love for the Lord continues to inspire my heart. I pray that this resource will serve others with the same spirit in which you live out each week.

TABLE OF CONTENTS

A LETTER FROM THE PASTOR | 9

CHAPTER 1: | 13
GOD'S DESIGN FOR CHURCH LEADERSHIP

CHAPTER 2: | 23
WHAT IS A TRUSTEE? AND WHAT IT ISN'T?

CHAPTER 3: | 33
FOLLOWING PASTORAL LEADERSHIP

CHAPTER 4: | 43
A HEART OF SERVANT LEADERSHIP

CHAPTER 5: | 55
PROTECTING THE MINISTRY LOGISTICALLY

CHAPTER 6: | 71
FINANCIAL INTEGRITY AND TRANSPARENCY

CHAPTER 7: | 89
TEAMWORK AND UNITY WITH CHURCH LEADERSHIP

CHAPTER 8: | 107
LEGAL AND ETHICAL RESPONSIBILITY

CHAPTER 9: | 123
GROWING SPIRITUALLY IN THE ROLE

CHAPTER 10: | 139
FAITHFULNESS IN THE BACKGROUND

A LETTER FROM THE AUTHOR...
TO THE MAN WILLING TO BE TRUSTED WITH THE TASK

Dear Brother in Christ,

If you're reading this, it's because you've either answered the call to serve as a trustee or are prayerfully considering it. Either way, I want to express my gratitude.

You may not feel qualified. You may even wonder, *"Why me?"* But God often calls men not because they have all the answers, but because they are willing to serve faithfully. He's not looking for men of status. He's looking for stewards.

Being a church trustee is not a role most people see or understand. It's quiet. It's behind the scenes. But make no mistake, its impact reaches into the very heart of the church's ministry. What happens publicly in a church is often sustained by what happens privately, through the faithfulness of men like you.

This book was born out of that very truth. As a pastor and church planter, I've seen what happens when trustees serve well and, sadly, what happens when they don't.

That's why this isn't a book of policy or procedure. Those things vary from church to church and pastor to pastor. Every local church has the freedom and responsibility to set its own structures, expectations, and systems.

Instead, this book is about biblical principles and truths that transcend man-made preferences and programs. It's about the heart of the trustee, the stewardship of the role, and the spirit of unity that protects the health of the church. These chapters will help you walk in wisdom, humility, and accountability as you support your pastor and serve your congregation.

You've been entrusted with more than tasks; you've been entrusted with the integrity and testimony of a local New Testament church. That's no small assignment. It demands character, spiritual maturity, faithfulness, and a spirit of grace. My prayer is that this book will help you grow in all of those areas.

So, whether you serve in a small country church or a growing urban ministry, know this: you matter, your role matters, and the way you carry yourself in this role can either strengthen or strain the work of God in your church.

Let these chapters be a help to you. Read them slowly, think deeply, and pray often. Let them remind you that your greatest strength is not in control, but in character. Not in making decisions, but in protecting what matters most.

Thank you for stepping into the responsibility. Thank you for protecting your pastor, your church, and your testimony. And thank you for being willing to be trusted with the task.

God Bless,

Pastor Steven Pratt, Jr.
FaithWay Bible Baptist Church
Calgary, Alberta, Canada

"This book exists to call trustees to a higher standard of faithful stewards who serve under pastoral leadership, protect the integrity of the church, and carry the weight of ministry with humility, wisdom, and grace."

Pastor Steven Pratt, Jr.

Chapter 1
God's Design for Church Leadership

I remember the early days of my spiritual journey when I was asked to serve as a trustee in my local church. I didn't fully understand what it meant. I thought it might just involve helping out more, maybe taking on some extra responsibility. My heart was surrendered, and I was willing to serve, but looking back, I didn't understand how that role fit within God's design for the church.

And that's where we should begin. Before we discuss the role of trustees, we need to first understand how God structured His church. Because if we don't have the right foundation, we'll build everything else on the wrong assumptions.

Before we begin, consider the following questions. *What do you believe God's design is for how a church should be led? Who leads? Who serves? How are decisions made? What matters most in leadership?*

In the pages ahead, we'll answer these questions, not from tradition or opinion, but from Scripture.

And once we understand how God designed leadership to function, we'll better understand where the trustee fits into that structure.

That's important because, for many trustees, we accept the role, we mean well, and our hearts are willing, but we don't always understand what we've stepped into.

So, before we discuss the trustee, let's take a step back. Let's start where God starts, with the design of the church itself. Because when we understand how God structured leadership in His church, we'll see more clearly where your role fits in.

God's Leadership Structure

God has clearly outlined the structure of His church. In the New Testament, we see pastors (also referred to as elders or bishops) given the responsibility to lead, feed, and oversee the flock (1 Peter 5:2; Acts 20:28; 1 Timothy 3:1–7). They are accountable to Christ and will one day give an account for the souls under their care.

To assist them, the church appoints deacons, spiritual men chosen by the congregation to serve the physical and practical needs of the body, so that the pastors can give themselves to prayer and the ministry of the Word (Acts 6:2–4; Philippians 1:1; 1 Timothy 3:8–13).

And while the Bible doesn't name trustees as an official office, their function is a biblical one. Trustees are responsible for helping to steward the legal, financial, and logistical aspects of church life. They operate under pastoral leadership, often in coordination with deacons, and serve as faithful protectors of what God is doing in and through the church.

In fact, there's a biblical word that perfectly describes what a trustee is meant to be, and that word is steward. In Scripture, the word *"steward"* describes someone who faithfully manages what belongs to another (Luke 12:42; Titus 1:7). That's the heart of what a trustee is called to do.

You are entrusted with the oversight of the church's practical matters, its property, its facilities, and its legal and financial standing, but all of these still belong to the Lord. So, the fundamental role of a Trustee is a steward. That means this job isn't about power or position. It's about faithful service.

The Book of Acts provides a vivid picture of how the early church operated. In Acts 6, a practical problem arose: certain widows were being neglected in the daily ministry.

The apostles recognized the issue but didn't try to handle everything themselves. Instead, they called on the church to choose spiritually qualified men who could attend to the practical needs, allowing the apostles to stay focused on prayer and the ministry of the Word.

This moment in Acts 6 is commonly understood as the appointment of the first deacons, not trustees. However, the principle still applies. The apostles didn't surrender their spiritual authority, but they did delegate responsibility to faithful men.

Similarly, while trustees are not deacons or pastors, they are appointed to help bear the load of practical responsibilities within the church. It is essential to remember that trustees do not replace the spiritual offices outlined in Scripture, but they serve in a way that supports them.

The principle in Acts 6 remains as relevant today as it was then: pastors and local churches need trustworthy men who can handle practical matters. Trustees fill that need, not by stepping into a spiritual office, but by faithfully serving in a supporting role.

Acts 6:3–4 says:

"Wherefore, brethren, look ye out among you seven men of honest report, full of the Holy Ghost and wisdom, whom we may appoint over this business. But we will give ourselves continually to prayer, and to the ministry of the word."

This text teaches us a valuable lesson: spiritual leaders require trustworthy individuals to assist in managing day-to-day tasks, thereby enabling the church to function smoothly. While trustees are not spiritual leaders, they play a vital role in freeing the pastor to focus on the spiritual oversight of the church.

Now, I know what you might be thinking: *"But this passage is about selecting deacons, not trustees."* And you're right. These verses are specifically about deacons, but the lesson of spiritually guided selection applies to any position of service in the church. Just as the early church took time to seek out the right men, we too should take time to pray and seek God's direction when appointing trustees.

Not just anyone should be asked to serve in this role. A pastor shouldn't walk up to someone and say, *"Hey, do you want to be a trustee?"* We should prayerfully consider who is spiritually mature, faithful in their walk, and aligned with the mission of the church. Trustees may not hold a spiritual office, but they carry spiritual weight. They help protect the testimony, structure, and unity of the church.

That's why we must be careful about who serves in this role.

Trustees are not called to run the church; they're called to protect and support what God is doing in the church through its biblical leadership. That's why we are careful about who serves in this role. Trustees must be men of good character, faithful in their walk with God, and fully aligned with the church's mission and doctrine.

You're not just carrying a title, you're carrying trust. You're carrying the testimony of the church. And you're helping create stability so the work of God can move forward with clarity and confidence.

In our church, trustees are not staff. They don't make spiritual decisions, and they don't override the authority of the pastor. But they are vital. They carry out the practical decisions of the church. They are eyes and ears for the pastor.

They are an extension of stewardship, accountability, and wise counsel. And in that, they bring great strength to the church body.

This is where being both a pastor and a missionary has been a blessing. While on deputation, I have visited many churches and observed how they select, train, and empower their staff, deacons, and trustees. And I've seen it all, including the good, the bad, and the ugly.

I've seen both trustees and deacons try to take over the ministry, inserting themselves into leadership and bypassing the pastor.

I've also seen churches completely handcuffed because their trustees refused to engage, refusing to carry the weight of the work and forcing the pastor to do it all.

So let me share something vital, especially if you're considering becoming a trustee: **Help your pastor.**

He needs more help than he lets on. There's so much going through his mind at any given moment that he can't possibly think of everything. That's where you come in.

But help him with humility. Be meek. Be gentle. Don't say, *"Pastor, I'm doing this."* Ask him. Respect the order. The last thing he needs is to worry about whether someone is getting ahead of him, or around him. What he needs is a faithful man by his side who says, *"Pastor, I've got this covered, unless you'd rather go a different direction."*

And let me say this, when you serve like that, your pastor notices. The church notices. But most importantly, the Lord sees it. Your quiet faithfulness becomes a foundation that the whole ministry stands on.

You may not preach sermons or teach classes. You may never be known by title or applause. But when you protect the church, uphold your pastor, and serve with a willing spirit, you are fulfilling a role that strengthens everything God is building in that place.

And when you stand before the Lord, He won't ask how many meetings you attended. He'll look for faithfulness. Be the kind of man your pastor can trust and the kind of man God can reward.

As we move forward in this book, remember this: a trustee is not defined by what they control but by what they protect. You protect the mission, the resources, and the testimony of the church. And that's no small task.

**Let a man be found faithful.
That's our goal.**

What We've Learned in This Chapter

In this opening chapter, we take a step back to examine the broader picture of God's design for leadership in the local church. We learned that pastors and deacons are the two scriptural offices established in the New Testament. Pastors are called to lead, feed, and care for the flock. Deacons are called to serve alongside them, helping meet practical needs. Trustees are not a third office, but that doesn't make their role any less valuable.

We also discovered that while trustees are not spiritual leaders, their calling is deeply spiritual. They are stewards, faithful managers of the practical responsibilities that keep the church moving forward. Though the title isn't found in Scripture, the function is biblical. Trustees serve under pastoral leadership to protect the mission, manage the resources, and uphold the integrity of the church.

The story in Acts 6 reminded us that ministry thrives when spiritual leaders stay focused on prayer and the

Word, and faithful men step up to handle the day-to-day responsibilities. Trustees are not called to take over, they're called to come alongside. They are not decision-makers in the spiritual direction of the church, but they are defenders of its stability and order.

Finally, we learned that the heart of a trustee is the heart of a servant. This isn't about authority. It's about accountability. It's about seeing a need, carrying a burden, and supporting your pastor with humility, consistency, and strength. The best trustees aren't the loudest, they're the ones who can be trusted.

Chapter 2
What Is a Trustee? And What It Isn't?

Congratulations! You've been elected as one of your church's trustees, but now what?

You're not alone if you don't feel fully prepared. Most men don't. That's because stepping into this role is a step of faith. And that's okay. Embrace the newness and be willing to learn. You're not the first man to enter this position with more questions than answers.

Let me also say thank you, thank you for taking the time to read this book. Most trustees won't. But the fact that you are already seeking clarity tells me something about you: you care. And that willingness to be faithful, teachable, and dependable is exactly what this role requires.

Before a man can serve well as a trustee, he needs to understand exactly what the role is and, just as importantly, what it isn't. One of the most common sources of confusion in the church today is when roles get blurred. That's when problems arise. When trustees begin thinking like pastors or when churches run like corporations rather than congregations, the biblical design breaks down. Let's take time to clarify this role through a biblical lens.

First, we need to acknowledge something: the term *"trustee"* does not appear in Scripture. That doesn't make it unbiblical, but it does mean that we must be careful to define the role in a way that *supports* Scripture, not contradicts it.

So, what does that mean for you?

It means we need to be honest about what a trustee is and what it isn't. Not every good man is called to preach. Not every faithful man is called to pastor or serve as a deacon. But every role in the church has a biblical pattern and purpose.

Let's begin by looking at the biblical structure of leadership and where trustees do not fit, so we can better understand where they do.

TRUSTEES ARE NOT SPIRITUAL LEADERS

The Bible gives spiritual authority to pastors (also referred to as elders or bishops) and appoints deacons as servant-leaders. These are the two scriptural offices of the local church.

Where confusion often sets in is when people assume that trustees are a third biblical office. They're not. Trustees are not spiritual overseers, nor are they ordained to preach or teach. While trustees should be spiritually mature men, their role is not to guide the church spiritually; that's the pastor's job.

As **Hebrews 13:17** says:

"Obey them that have the rule over you, and submit yourselves: for they watch for your souls, as they that must give account..."

According to Scripture, it is the pastor who will give an account to God for the spiritual health of the church. Trustees do not carry that responsibility, and they shouldn't carry that authority either.

That being said, serving as a trustee is a great way to test a calling to greater spiritual leadership, whether to the office of a deacon or even pastoral ministry. The Bible teaches that deacons must first be proved (1 Tim 3:10), and that a pastor must not be a novice (1 Tim 3:6). This role gives a man the opportunity to grow in humility, maturity, and practical responsibility, all while learning to serve under pastoral leadership.

I know this because it was my path as well. I didn't start out as a pastor. I first served as a trustee. I didn't know everything, but I was willing. And over time, God used that season to stretch me, shape me, and prepare me for what was next. That's why I take this role so seriously. It's not just a title. It's a training ground.

So remember, as a trustee, you won't be leading spiritually, but you will be learning how to serve faithfully. You'll learn what it means to come alongside your pastor, to protect the church, and to carry part of the load with wisdom and grace.

Having settled what this role is not meant to be, we can now focus on what it is: a vital, God-honoring role that supports the church in powerful and practical ways.

Legal and Operational Stewards

The role of a trustee is practical. They help the church fulfill its legal obligations, manage its property, protect its assets, and ensure that things are done decently and in order. A trustee might be asked to review contracts, work with landlords or city officials, approve purchases, or oversee maintenance. These are necessary tasks that allow the ministry to operate smoothly and safely.

Paul wrote in **Romans 13:7:**

"Render therefore to all their dues: tribute to whom tribute is due; custom to whom custom; fear to whom fear; honour to whom honour."

This reminds us that even spiritual institutions, such as the church, operate within a legal framework. Trustees help the church fulfill its obligations with integrity, without ever allowing legal matters to supersede biblical principles.

Trustees Help, Not Hinder

If you're a trustee, please don't just stand around and watch your pastor do all the work in the church.

What do I mean? I've seen it too many times: trustees huddled in a corner chatting, while no one is greeting guests, the trash is overflowing, and the pastor is down on his knees taping cables, setting up chairs, and doing everything he can to avoid getting overwhelmed before preaching.

Friend, this needs to be said: open your eyes and stay in a constant state of readiness for the ministry. Your pastor shouldn't be running from one task to the next. He should be walking the room, connecting with people, studying his notes, and preparing to deliver the Word.

Instead, when trustees fail to step up, he's doing your job and falling short in his. I think we can both agree that there's not much spiritual about taping cables.

Meanwhile, someone might walk in who needs prayer. A first-time visitor may go unnoticed. A hurting family might miss their moment of encouragement, because the pastor was too busy wrestling with the sound system.

Your pastor isn't always going to come over and tell you what needs to be done, he's hoping you'll already see it and take action. And when you do, please, do it right. Don't rush it. Don't take shortcuts. Because here's the reality: if he has to go back and fix what you started, that's not helping, it's doubling his load.

And he's not ignoring you if he doesn't explain why something needs to be done a certain way. He simply doesn't have the time in that moment to walk you through all the reasons. He just needs it done right, the first time, so he can stay focused on the spiritual work God has called him to do.

And here's how your pastor sees it: if he can't trust you with the small things, like a simple setup or task, how can he trust you with anything bigger? It's not about perfection; it's about dependability. Every unfinished or poorly done job sends a silent message that says, *"You'll still have to handle it, Pastor."* That wears on him. It chips away at trust.

While I was a trustee, I watched my pastor approach men and ask them to do something, such as watch the door and greet guests, only to see that person sitting in their seat five minutes later, just ten minutes before the service was set to start. Do you know what that communicates to your pastor?

He trusted you to do a task, and now he's wondering if he can trust you with anything else. Faithfulness requires you to be faithful in the little things. It might seem small to you, but to him, it's one more weight added right before he steps into the pulpit. And I'll tell you from experience, it's hard to preach with a burdened heart because someone didn't take a simple responsibility seriously.

But when you step in, do it right, and do it without being asked, it doesn't go unnoticed. It tells your pastor, *"You're not in this alone."*

Support the Pastor, Not Replace Him

Some churches operate as if their board of trustees serves as a governing body that votes and determines the direction of the church. That may be common in some denominational structures, but it is not biblical. In a biblical church, the pastor leads under the headship of Christ, and the church body affirms decisions prayerfully and corporately.

Trustees in our church don't vote against the pastor. They walk alongside him. They don't set the spiritual direction; they help carry out what's already been decided. That doesn't mean they're *"yes men,"* they should be wise counselors, offering insight and accountability. However, their authority stems from the church body and is exercised under the guidance of pastoral leadership.

A Word of Caution

Problems arise when trustees believe they have authority *over* the pastor, or when they forget that their role is one of stewardship, not control. We've all heard of churches split or pastors pushed out by boards that forgot their place. That's not biblical. And that's not FaithWay.

In our church, trustees serve in submission to Christ, under the leadership of the pastor, and in partnership with one another. That's a healthy, God-honoring structure.

What We've Learned in This Chapter

In this chapter, we defined what a trustee is and, just as importantly, what a trustee is not. Trustees are not spiritual leaders. That responsibility belongs to the pastor, who has been called and ordained to oversee the spiritual health of the church, and to deacons, who serve alongside him in meeting the needs of the people. Trustees may be spiritual men, but their role is not to guide the church spiritually. Their calling is different.

We also learned that the role of a trustee is deeply practical. It's not about position or recognition, it's about stewardship. Trustees help the church fulfill legal obligations, care for its property, manage financial responsibilities, and ensure that the ministry can function smoothly. These are not minor tasks. They are vital to the work of the church, and when done faithfully, they enable the pastor to focus on prayer, preaching, and shepherding.

We've seen that trustees are meant to help, not hinder. When a trustee steps up, sees a need, and takes action without being asked, he becomes an extension of the pastor's hands and heart. On the other hand, when trustees are passive, disorganized, or unreliable, they become one more burden that weighs the pastor down right before he steps into the pulpit. Dependability matters. Excellence matters. Showing up, staying ready, and doing things well, those things make all the difference.

Lastly, we've been reminded that this is a role of stewardship, not control. Trustees don't run the church. They don't vote against the pastor or take the lead on spiritual matters. They serve in submission to Christ, under the leadership of the pastor, and in alignment with the church body. That's where true strength lies in unity, humility, and faithfulness.

As the Bible says, *"Moreover it is required in stewards, that a man be found faithful"* (1 Corinthians 4:2). That's the calling. That's the aim. Trustees should be found faithful.

Chapter 3
Following Pastoral Leadership

Looking back on my time as a trustee, I remember a moment when I didn't fully understand my pastor's vision. We were sitting in a meeting, and he was doing his best to explain what the Lord had laid on his heart. But if I'm being honest, it didn't make much sense to me at the time. I couldn't see the full picture. Still, I could see something even more important, the passion in his eyes and the burden he carried while trying to cast that vision to us.

Now, at that time, I was working as a systems engineer. If you don't know me, let me just say this: I'm a detailed person. That's how my brain works. I like to see all the steps, the process, and the plan. I want to understand how point A leads to point B, and how that gets us to point C. So, when my pastor shared a vision that felt more like a burden than a blueprint, it left me feeling unsure.

But here's what I had to realize: The vision wasn't his, it was from the Lord. And he was sharing it with us the best way he could.

My job in that moment wasn't to critique the plan. It wasn't to say no just because I couldn't see the end result. My job was to help bring the vision to fruition. To take what God had placed on my pastor's heart and do everything I could to support it, not slow it down. The last thing I ever wanted to do was become a stumbling block to the work of God.

And now, having served as a pastor myself, I see that moment with fresh eyes. I understand that burden far more deeply. When God gives a pastor a vision, it's often bigger than the words we know how to use. We try to explain it, but we're still wrapping our minds around it, too. What we need in those moments isn't a panel of skeptics; we need men of faith who say, *"Pastor, I may not fully see it yet, but I'm with you."*

That moment stuck with me. It shaped how I served as a trustee. And now, as a pastor, I've come to realize how crucial that kind of support really is. Trustees don't always need to see the full picture. But they do need to trust that their pastor is following the Lord. That's what this chapter is all about: understanding your role in relation to the pastor's leadership and choosing to follow with faith, not friction.

If the local church is a body, then Christ is the Head, and under Him, He gives pastors to serve as under-shepherds to lead the flock. This is not a suggestion or a tradition; it's God's design. And when it comes to the role of a trustee, everything hinges on understanding and respecting that order.

In our church, we don't believe in a board-run church. We believe in a pastor-led church. That doesn't mean the pastor is a dictator, nor does it mean he works alone. However, it does mean that God has placed the pastor in a position of spiritual authority, and the rest of us, including trustees, serve to support, not override, that leadership.

The Biblical Role of the Pastor

Let's look at **Hebrews 13:17** again:

"Obey them that have the rule over you, and submit yourselves: for they watch for your souls, as they that must give account..."

This verse puts a weight on the pastor that trustees do not carry. The pastor will stand before God and give an account for how he led the church. That's a sobering truth. It also makes it clear that no one else, not a trustee, not a committee, not even a congregation, carries that same level of responsibility.

That's why trustees must approach their service with humility and clarity. You are not watching over souls; you are helping create the structure so that the one who *is* watching over souls can do it faithfully and without distraction.

Trustees Are Counselors, Not Controllers

There's great wisdom in surrounding the pastor with faithful men who can offer counsel, experience, and support.

Proverbs 11:14 says:

"Where no counsel is, the people fall: but in the multitude of counsellors there is safety."

But there's a difference between counseling and controlling. Trustees must never confuse offering input with making decisions that belong to the pastor. The pastor leads the ministry. Trustees help guard the structure that allows him to do it well.

As a pastor now, I can tell you it's not the weight of preaching that breaks a man. It's the feeling of standing alone. I've seen firsthand how one faithful trustee can make a difference between a pastor pressing on or quietly burning out.

That's why the right kind of support means more than most people realize, and it's exactly the kind of support we see in the next example.

Moses and His Helpers

In Exodus 18, we find a moment that every spiritual leader can relate to. Moses was overwhelmed. The needs of the people were constant. From sunrise to sunset, he sat judging, settling disputes, and trying to carry the full weight of a nation's burdens alone.

His father-in-law, Jethro, watched all this and spoke with clarity and compassion:

"Thou wilt surely wear away... this thing is too heavy for thee; thou art not able to perform it thyself alone." **Exodus 18:18**

Moses wasn't failing because he lacked faith; he was failing because he lacked help. And that's the principle we need to see, even God-ordained leaders need support.

Jethro didn't tell Moses to hand over the reins. He didn't suggest a new system of power or leadership. He simply said, *"Let others help you carry the weight."* That's the role of a trustee. Not to lead instead of the pastor, but to make sure the pastor doesn't wear out trying to lead alone.

Can I just say this gently? I've seen good pastors burn out not because they were lazy or unspiritual, but because they were alone. They were doing the work of five men with no one beside them. Not because no one was around, but because no one stepped up. Often, the leadership was just a step away, watching, talking, unaware.

And sometimes all it would've taken was one faithful man. One trustee who said, *"Pastor, I've got this. You focus on what you need to do."*

That's the Jethro principle in action, not control, not criticism, but commitment to help. When trustees follow that model, the church flourishes and the pastor finishes his race without collapsing under the weight.

That's what a trustee is called to do: not to lead for the pastor, but to lighten the load so he can lead well. Jethro wasn't introducing a chain of command; he was teaching shared responsibility. And when a trustee steps into that role with humility and faithfulness, it changes everything.

Unity with the Pastor

There will be times when you may not fully understand every decision the pastor makes, and that's okay. What matters most in those moments is trust. A trustee must trust the pastor's heart, trust his calling, and trust that God is leading him. That kind of unity doesn't come from voting; it comes from walking in the Spirit.

Amos 3:3 asks, *"Can two walk together, except they be agreed?"* As a trustee, it is your duty to seek agreement, not to challenge leadership, but to strengthen it.

And let me tell you, the devil knows how powerful that kind of unity is. That's exactly why he tries to destroy it. It breaks my heart to think how many times Satan has sown seeds of discord to damage or divide a church.

You see, Satan doesn't need to blow the doors off a church to stop it. All he has to do is wedge a little distance between the pastor and his men. And before you know it, you have a divided leadership team. A little misunderstanding here, a little offence there, and add a lack of communication, and you have a recipe for division.

I've seen pastors wear out, not because they didn't love the ministry, but because they felt alone in it. Not because no one was around, but because no one stepped up with them.

Like I mentioned earlier, it only takes one faithful trustee to make all the difference. One voice saying, *"Pastor, I've got your back. Let me take that off your plate,"* might be what keeps him going in the hardest of seasons. That's what unity looks like.

But here's the other side. Sometimes, the pastor might miss something. He might move too fast. He might unintentionally hurt you.

So what do you do?

You stay humble, you don't gossip, and you don't distance yourself. You go to him, not to confront him, but to get clarity.

That kind of unity is mature, it's spiritual, and it's the kind of unity that builds a strong, healthy church. One that Satan can not destroy.

So don't just guard the building, guard your relationship with the pastor. Because when unity between a pastor and trustee is strong, the church becomes unshakable.

WHAT WE'VE LEARNED IN THIS CHAPTER

If there's one thing I hope you've taken from this chapter, it's that your pastor doesn't need a board; he needs brothers. Men who will stand beside him, not over him. Men who understand that leadership in the church isn't about control, it's about carrying the weight together.

We saw that following pastoral leadership doesn't mean you'll always understand every detail, but it does mean you choose to trust. Not blindly, but faithfully. You trust the man God's put in place. And even if the plan isn't clear to you yet, you don't pull back, you lean in.

We examined the example of Moses and Jethro and saw how crucial it is for leaders to have support. Moses wasn't failing in faith; he was just carrying too much alone. And that's what your pastor faces more than you realize. He's not asking you to take over; he just needs you to step in and say, *"You don't have to do it all alone."*

And let's not ignore this: Satan is after your church. He doesn't have to split the whole thing down the middle; he just needs to put a little space between the pastor and his men. A little offence. A little silence. A little misread moment. That's all it takes. But unity? Real, God-honoring unity? That shuts the door on division. That protects the whole flock.

Sometimes that unity means choosing to trust when things feel unclear. Other times, it means choosing humility when you're hurt. Either way, it's worth fighting for. Because when unity is strong, the church is strong.

So, here's the question I want to leave you with: *Can your pastor count on you?* Not just when things are clear, but when they're not. Not just when it's easy, but when it's heavy.

Because when a trustee chooses faith, chooses support, and chooses unity, the whole church feels it. Souls are reached, visitors are welcomed, and hurting families are helped.

That's what's at stake. This is more than leadership, it's about eternity. So, stay faithful. Stay aligned. And remember, when you support your pastor, you're helping carry the gospel to someone who's still waiting to hear it.

Chapter 4:
A Heart of Servant Leadership

I look forward to the day when our church deacons and trustees handle all the setup and teardown for each service. Not because I don't want to do it, but because it will give me the time to connect with the people and prepare to preach.

As I write this book, FaithWay Bible Baptist Church Calgary is still a baby church that God is growing mightily. Every week is amazing. We don't go a single service without seeing God's hand at work. It's truly a blessing.

But I do look forward to the day when the church can start walking without my help in all the practical things.

I'll be honest, there are times I feel overwhelmed trying to get everything ready before the service. And that pressure does carry over into the service. Even though I try not to let it show, I feel as though I'm being rushed. And when I feel rushed, I tend to rush the service too. I've missed announcements, I've skipped over a special, and I've been distracted when I should have been focused.

I'll never forget the day, back when I served as a trustee and later as a deacon, when our pastor walked into the church and everything was already ready. You could see the relief in his posture, and you could hear the difference in his tone and delivery. He wasn't worn out from stress; he was ready to preach, and it showed!

Not only was the preaching stronger, but the church also began to grow. He had time to build a connection with first-time visitors, and as a result, more people were saved. You see, the time he had been spending setting up was time taken from connecting with the people. But now, he could focus on ministry, before and after the service.

That moment taught me something I'll never forget. Sometimes, the most spiritual thing a man can do is stack chairs or set up a sound system if it means freeing up his pastor to reach people. Because when you serve behind the scenes with the right heart, the whole church feels it. And that is the purpose of this chapter.

If there's one trait that defines a biblical trustee, it's not business savvy or years of experience. It's not education or personality. It's a servant's heart.

That may sound simple, but it's profound and *rare*. In a world where leadership often means control, power, and status, Jesus gave us a very different model. He said the greatest leader is the greatest servant. That principle is just as true for a trustee as it is for a pastor or deacon.

The Example of Christ

Philippians 2:3–8 gives us the blueprint:

"Let nothing be done through strife or vainglory; but in lowliness of mind let each esteem other better than themselves... Let this mind be in you, which was also in Christ Jesus... and took upon him the form of a servant."

That's the standard. Not corporate leadership, not positional authority, but Christlike humility.

As a trustee, you are not leading from a platform. You're leading from the background. And it's not always easy. But it is necessary.

What Kind of Man Should a Trustee Be?

Now, this can vary from church to church. That's because the Bible doesn't give direct qualifications for trustees like it does for pastors or deacons. But that doesn't mean we make decisions without biblical wisdom.

In many cases, churches will use the same qualifications outlined for deacons, except for certain areas, such as the marriage requirement, especially in cases where a faithful man may not be qualified to serve as a deacon due to a past divorce. The trustee role can be a great place for him to serve with integrity and still be used by God in a meaningful way.

Ultimately, the selection of trustees should be a decision made prayerfully by the pastor and the church. It's not just about filling a position, it's about placing the right men in place to protect the ministry, support the leadership, and walk in spiritual maturity.

Here's what we look for:

- Faithful in church attendance and grounded in sound doctrine.

- Spiritually mature and actively growing.

- Honest in character and trustworthy with responsibility.

- Fully support the pastor and the church's mission.

- Live above reproach in their public and private testimony.

Titus 2:7 says:

"In all things shewing thyself a pattern of good works: in doctrine shewing uncorruptness, gravity, sincerity."

That's what we're looking for, not just a body or someone who can help, but someone whose life reflects spiritual strength and integrity. A trustee isn't chosen simply because they are available. He's chosen because he's dependable and because he carries himself in a way that honors Christ.

And once we understand what kind of man a trustee should be, we can better appreciate how his unseen faithfulness lays the groundwork for spiritual fruit in the church.

BEHIND-THE-SCENES BUT NOT UNSEEN

There's a unique weight to this role. A lot of your work will be unnoticed by most of the church. People may not see the building repairs, the financial meetings, or the paperwork you help process. But God sees it. And more than that, your faithfulness creates a foundation for ministry to flourish.

You're helping the church function with order, credibility, and integrity. That might not feel spiritual, but it absolutely is.

Colossians 3:23–24 reminds us:

"And whatsoever ye do, do it heartily, as to the Lord, and not unto men... for ye serve the Lord Christ."

If you sweep a floor, fix a door, review a lease, or balance a budget, all for the Lord, it becomes worship.

Here's the truth: People may never notice what you do when everything is done right, but they'll absolutely notice when it's not. A flickering light, a dirty chair, or fingerprints on a wall are the things that can distract a visitor from what matters most.

As a pastor, my heart is for every person who walks through the doors to leave refreshed by the Lord, not laughing about what they saw or frustrated by what was missing. We're not trying to impress them, but we're trying to remove distractions so that the message of Christ can be heard clearly.

Because when a visitor leaves our church, I don't want their conversation to be about how dusty the chairs were, I want it to be about how deeply God spoke to their heart.

That's where you come in, not just with a servant's hands, but with a servant's heart. One that cares not only about the practical, but also about the spiritual. Because this isn't just about cleaning or fixing, it's about creating the kind of environment where the Holy Spirit is free to move without distraction, division, or disorder.

And sometimes, protecting that environment means more than setting up chairs. It means standing guard over the heart of the church.

A Servant Who Protects

One of your jobs as a trustee is to protect the church. That doesn't just mean fixing things or watching over finances. It also means protecting the unity and health of the body. If someone tries to stir up gossip, sow division, or disrespect pastoral authority, you must stand for what is right, even if it's uncomfortable.

A servant doesn't just serve quietly; he also serves

courageously. Sometimes that means being the one who steps in with grace and strength when others step back in silence.

As Paul reminded the church in Corinth:

"Watch ye, stand fast in the faith, quit you like men, be strong." **1 Corinthians 16:13**

That's trustee-level strength. Not loud, not controlling, but steady, watchful, faithful, and strong. Exactly what the church needs. Exactly what God honors.

Imagine a trustee or any member of the leadership team who sees division starting and says nothing. How do you think that impacts the spirit of the church? What message does that send to the pastor? To the people? More importantly, what does it say to God?

We must be on guard. Not just against what's obvious, but against what's subtle, like whispers, rolled eyes, unresolved offences. Satan loves to slip in through the cracks of silence and inaction. And make no mistake, he's not just attacking personalities, he's attacking God's work.

Or worse... imagine a trustee who shares private matters that were meant to stay between them and their pastor. Conversations that should have been taken to God in prayer now become fuel for gossip. That kind of breach doesn't just cause hurt; it causes spiritual damage. It breaks trust, poisons the unity of the body, and grieves the Holy Spirit.

God is not indifferent to these things. He sees. He hears. He knows the intentions of every heart.

Christ is honored when His church is protected, when men stand, not just to serve with their hands, but to guard with their words, their actions, and their integrity. That's what it means to lead well. That's what it means to serve in the fear of God.

So, ask yourself this:

Am I guarding the pastor's back or opening the door to criticism? Am I a shield or a sponge? When God looks at my stewardship, my spirit, my silence, my strength, can He say, *"That's a man I can trust to protect My house"*?

Because the real question is never just *"Can I do the job?"* It's *"Can God trust me with the weight of it?"*

That's the call of a servant who protects. One who fears the Lord, honors His church, and strengthens the hands of the man of God. When you serve like that, He sees it, He rewards it, and the church is better for it.

What We've Learned in This Chapter

If there's one truth we can't miss, it's this: God isn't looking for trustees with titles. He's looking for men with towels. Men who are willing to serve, sacrifice, and strengthen the work of God behind the scenes.

We learned that servant leadership isn't about stepping up to be seen; it's about stepping down to lift others up. It's about saying, *"Whatever I can do to help the gospel go forward, I'm in."* When trustees serve with that heart, the entire church feels it. And more than that, God blesses it.

We saw that a trustee's qualifications aren't just about ability, but character. And we were reminded that unseen work is not unnoticed by God.

Then we learned that a trustee's job is more than practical. It's also spiritual. You're not just guarding the building, you're helping guard the unity of the body. That means standing against gossip, protecting the pastor's reputation, and walking in humility, courage, and integrity.

So, here's the challenge: don't just be a worker, be a worshipper while you work. Don't just be reliable, be faithful. Don't just be available, be trustworthy.

Because when God finds a trustee like that, souls are saved, churches are strengthened, and the pastor can press forward with courage, knowing he's not carrying the burden alone.

That's the kind of man God can use.
That's the kind of servant every church needs.
And That's the kind of trustee you're called to be.

Chapter 5:
Protecting the Ministry Logistically

One of the most overlooked ministries in the church is the ministry of making a good first impression. What do I mean by that?

I once heard a seasoned pastor say something I'll never forget: *"We didn't lose people because of preaching. We lost them because the lawn never got mowed."*

At first, I thought he was joking. However, he continued to explain how his church had experienced a powerful season of growth. People were being saved, the preaching was strong, and the spirit in the church was sweet. But behind the scenes, the property was being neglected, week after week.

"We had the gospel right," he said, *"but the church looked like no one cared. And eventually, people believed that no one did."*

That stuck with me. Because while preaching reaches the heart, first impressions often determine whether someone ever returns to hear that message again.

You see, ministry doesn't begin in the pulpit. It begins in the parking lot. It begins when a visitor pulls onto the property, steps out of their car, and walks through the doors for the very first time.

The longer you've been in a church, the harder it is to see what visitors see. We grow used to the cracks in the sidewalk. We stop noticing the clutter in the corner. We don't smell the hallway anymore. But visitors do. And what they see, or don't see, shapes the tone of their visit before they ever hear the first song or open their Bible.

Our job isn't to impress. It's to remove distractions before they ever start.

And here's the thing: if we mow the grass, trim the weeds, and repair the sidewalk, nobody may notice. But that's the point. The best first impressions aren't always noticed; they're invisible. The only thing a visitor should focus on is the Word of God, not the water stains on the ceiling or the smell in the hallway.

That's why, as a trustee, you must learn to see with fresh eyes, with the eyes of someone walking in for the very first time.

Your job isn't just to mow the lawn or patch a wall. Your job is to protect the atmosphere of ministry. And it doesn't matter whether you rent the building or own it, it's still the Lord's House. It still matters. Because this isn't just about making a good impression. This is about creating a place where people come to meet with the Lord.

And when the place is clean, cared for, and ready, it shows the people we're ready too. When things look cared for, people feel cared for. And when people feel cared for, their hearts are more open to the truth.

That's why this chapter exists. Because someone has to care about these things. Someone has to see what others don't. Someone has to serve with fresh eyes and faithful hands.

And that someone is you.

As a trustee, you may never preach a sermon or lead a Bible study, but what you do enables those things to happen. When you take care of the physical, you're protecting the spiritual.

One of the most overlooked but vital aspects of church health is logistics. Every ministry needs a foundation to stand on, rooms to meet in, equipment to use, insurance for protection, contracts for rentals, and systems that keep everything running smoothly.

That's where trustees come in.

We're not talking about red tape or control; we're talking about stewardship. About making sure that the physical side of ministry reflects the seriousness of what God is doing in the spiritual.

When a guest walks into a clean, safe, well-kept church, they may not say anything. But when they walk into one that's neglected or falling apart, they may not hear anything else.

That's why God places trustees in the church. You may not preach the sermon or teach the class, but your hands make that ministry possible. When you cut the grass, clean the building, change the filters, repair the doors, or double-check a rental agreement, you are not just *"helping;"* you are protecting the church's ability to minister clearly, effectively, and without distraction.

So, while others may walk away from a service talking about the sermon or the music, God sees the man who was out there Saturday night fixing the irrigation or pulling weeds, making sure His house was ready.

Let All Things Be Done
Decently and in Order

The Apostle Paul gave us a clear and practical principle for the local church in **1 Corinthians 14:40**: *"Let all things be done decently and in order."*

While Paul was specifically addressing the structure of worship services, this principle extends to every part of church life, especially the behind-the-scenes work that most people never see. God values order. He is not the author of confusion. That means clean spaces matter. Functioning lights matter. Safe sidewalks and maintained rooms matter.

In the Old Testament, when God gave instructions for the tabernacle, every board, curtain, hook, and socket had a specific purpose. Nothing was random. Nothing was sloppy. Why? Because the environment where God's people met with Him was never meant to be an afterthought.

And it still isn't.

As a trustee, your ministry is to help ensure that our facilities reflect that kind of care and order. That means:

- The bathrooms are clean.
- The floors are vacuumed.
- The entryway is clear.

- The signage is helpful.
- The building is safe, well-lit, and inviting.

It's not glamorous. But it is godly.

If you've been around me long in ministry, you've probably heard me quote this verse more than once. I hold onto it tightly. As someone who's naturally drawn to structure and detail, I see the beauty and power of *"decently and in order."*

But it's not just a personality thing, it's a biblical thing. It's a spiritual conviction that spills into how we care for God's house.

Because here's the truth: when we keep things in order, we reflect the God of order. When our church is clean, safe, welcoming, and ready, it says something about the God we worship. It shows that we value His presence. That we're serious about His mission. And that we're doing all we can to remove distractions so people can focus on what really matters.

**But order isn't just about tidiness,
It's about stewardship.**

And that brings us to the next part of your calling as a trustee: not just maintaining order but faithfully managing what God has provided.

STEWARDING THE PROPERTY AND RESOURCES

Everything the church uses, including every chair, microphone, pulpit, cable, broom, vacuum, light switch, and lease agreement, has been provided by God through the giving of His people. That makes it sacred. Not in the mystical sense, but in the sense of stewardship. It's not just stuff. It's God's provision for the church.

And if God provided it, then He expects us to take care of it.

As a trustee, your role includes more than just noticing when something breaks. It's about staying alert. Watching for the slow leaks. Seeing what's starting to wear down. Recognizing what needs to be replaced *before* it becomes a problem. That's not just maintenance, it's ministry.

Here are some areas to stay aware of:

- **Repairs and Safety Hazards:** That loose handrail or uneven step might seem small until someone trips on it. Stewardship means addressing the small issues before they escalate into major problems. Walk the property, look for what others miss and fix what needs fixing.

- **Storage and Security:** If God's people entrust it to us, we should protect it. That means tools go back where they belong, doors get locked, and supplies stay stocked and orderly.

- **Fire Code and Liability Concerns:** Whether you rent or own the building, safety isn't optional. If a fire exit is blocked, a smoke detector is missing, or emergency lighting isn't working, it's not just a problem; it's a risk.

- **Warranties, Contracts, and Vendor Relationships:** Paperwork may not be exciting, but it becomes urgent the moment something breaks. Know where the warranties are. Keep contracts easy to find. Build good relationships with the people who service your equipment. When problems come, and they will, you'll be ready instead of scrambling.

You might not get thanked for catching a leak or fixing a latch, but if you don't, and it causes damage or risk, everyone will notice. Stewardship doesn't wait until something is a problem. It acts with foresight and care.

Let me ask you a question. How long has that light bulb been out?

Okay, you can call it a pet peeve of mine. But we often neglect to replace a light bulb that needs to be replaced because it may be too high, or perhaps we meant to address it after service, or maybe we didn't even notice.

Sure, it might not seem like a big deal to you, but stewardship isn't about what seems big. It's about being faithful with what's been placed in your care.

Luke 16:10 says,

"He that is faithful in that which is least is faithful also in much."

That light bulb is a stewardship test. So is the leaky faucet, the broken chair, and the back room that's slowly becoming a storage jungle. Because if it belongs to the church, it ultimately belongs to the Lord.

And if it belongs to the Lord, then it deserves our best attention, not our leftover energy.

Stewardship doesn't just fix what's broken; it anticipates what needs care. It doesn't say, *"Someone else will get to that."* It says, *"This is the Lord's house. I'll handle it."*

That's what trustees do. You don't just preserve the resources of the church; you protect the testimony behind them quietly, consistently, and faithfully.

That's why this role matters. If a church isn't well-stewarded on the physical side, it becomes a stumbling block to its spiritual mission. This causes people to get distracted, feelings get frustrated, and worst of all, it communicates that we care more about what we *say* than how we *serve*.

So don't wait until you're asked. Stay ahead! See the small things, fix the unnoticed things, and maintain what no one else is thinking about.

But stewardship doesn't stop at maintenance. It extends to how we support the ministry itself. Let's discuss how to make ministry possible, not complicated.

Making Ministry Possible, Not Complicated

One of the great dangers trustees face, without ever meaning to, is turning protection into obstruction. What starts as a desire to be careful can quietly become a habit of hesitation. And before long, the systems that were put in place to safeguard the church start making it harder for ministry to move forward.

That's not stewardship. That's red tape.

Let me be clear: stewardship is never about control, it's about clearing the way. You're not a gatekeeper keeping people out; you're a door holder, helping ministry leaders walk through.

You're not there to slow things down with endless questions and second-guessing. You're there to ask the right questions ahead of time, so the pastor doesn't have to. You're there to anticipate needs, solve problems, and make sure nothing's standing in the way when it's time to serve.

That means...

- If the children's ministry wants to use a room, make sure it's ready, not restricted.

- If the pastor needs to print flyers or access a tool, it shouldn't feel like he's breaking into a bank vault.

- If the team is planning a big outreach, don't just say, *"Let me check."* Say, *"Let me help."*

In other words, don't make ministry leaders climb over hurdles you were called to remove.

I know your heart is to protect the church. Mine is too. But protection and partnership go hand in hand. You're not just guarding the building, you're supporting the mission. You're not just watching the budget, you're fueling the ministry.

And when something can't be done, don't just say *"No."* Say, *"Not yet. But here's what we can do to get there."* Bring solutions, not roadblocks.

That's what trustees do when they understand their role.

Because ministry isn't powered by policies, it's

powered by people working together, under God's direction, with humility and clarity.

And when a pastor knows he has trustees who clear the way instead of clouding the process, he walks into each week with confidence. He knows the team isn't just behind him in title, they're beside him in action.

That's what makes ministry possible, not complicated.

Building Trust Through Excellence

Here's something every trustee needs to understand: <u>excellence builds trust</u>.

When a first-time guest walks into a church that's clean, prepared, and well-maintained, they may not even realize why they feel comfortable, but they do. The lighting feels intentional. The signage is clear. The seating is ready. The nursery looks safe. The building smells fresh. And without saying a word, those things whisper, *"We were expecting you."*

That kind of environment builds confidence, not just for visitors, but also among the people who serve.

- When the children's workers know the rooms are clean and stocked, they serve with joy.

- When the music team knows the sound system is ready, they lead with clarity.

- When the pastor walks in and everything is already in place, he preaches with focus.

Trust is built one act of faithfulness at a time. One repaired hinge, one updated schedule, and one light bulb changed before anyone noticed it was out.

You're not doing these things to be noticed; you're doing them so nothing else steals the attention from the message of Christ. And by that, you are setting the table for ministry. And when it's done with care, people sit down and receive what God has for them.

Proverbs 22:29 says,

"Seest thou a man diligent in his business? he shall stand before kings..."

Diligence opens doors, and practical excellence, done with consistency and humility, creates a culture where the ministry can thrive.

Because people don't return to churches that feel chaotic or uncared for. However, they do return to places where the gospel is clear, the spirit is sweet, and the details have been handled with grace.

That's what trustees make possible.

You may never know the full impact of a smooth Sunday. You may never hear the stories of the people who stayed because nothing got in the way of the message. But God knows. And your quiet, consistent faithfulness has eternal value.

What We've Learned in This Chapter

In this chapter, we've seen that trustees are not just caretakers of buildings; they're protectors of ministry.

We learned that ministry doesn't begin at the pulpit; it begins in the parking lot. The way a church looks, smells, and feels sets the tone long before a single verse is read or a word is preached. That means a light bulb, a patch of weeds, or a cluttered corner can either prepare the heart or distract it.

We saw that order matters to God. 1 Corinthians 14:40 calls us to do all things *"decently and in order."* That's not just about the worship service, it's about bathrooms that are clean, signage that's clear, and a space that's safe, welcoming, and ready.

We also discovered that stewardship isn't glamorous, but it is a godly practice. Everything in the church, from the chairs to the storage closet to the sound system, has been provided by God through His people. That means every item matters. It's not just about fixing what's broken; it's about seeing what's beginning to fail and stepping in before it does.

We learned that good trustees remove barriers, not create them. They make ministry easier, not harder. They don't get in the way of what God is doing; they help clear the path so others can run freely in the work of the gospel.

And finally, we were reminded that excellence builds trust. Not flashy, over-the-top, showy excellence, but the quiet kind. The faithful kind. The kind that says, *"We were expecting you."* And more importantly, *"We're serious about the message you've come to hear."*

So, here's the challenge: don't just do the work, own the responsibility. Don't just show up, stay ahead. Don't just repair, prepare.

Because when trustees steward the practical side of ministry with faithfulness and vision, it protects the spiritual side in ways we may never see until eternity.

And that's the kind of trustee the church needs.
That's the kind of servant the Lord blesses.
That's the kind of steward you're called to be.

Chapter 6:
Financial Integrity and Transparency

Let me ask you something important, and I mean this sincerely: *Do you give faithfully? Do you give of the tithe?* As a trustee, can you say with a clean conscience before the Lord, *"Yes, I tithe faithfully and cheerfully"*? Because if you're a trustee, that question isn't optional, it's essential!

Before you can effectively steward the church's finances, you must first be surrendered to your own giving. If you're going to lead the church practically, you must first lead spiritually by example. And one of the most visible, revealing signs of that is whether or not you're giving faithfully. Leadership must always set the example.

How can we, as the leaders entrusted to protect the resources of God's house, expect God's people to give in faith if we're not doing it ourselves?

I say that because I know what it's like to sit on the other side of this. Before I was called into the ministry, I was what I'd call a *"Casual Christian."* We attended church when it was convenient for us. And when that offering plate came around, we'd toss in a twenty and feel like we were being generous.

But the truth? We weren't giving... We were tipping.

We knew what the Bible said. We knew the tithe was 10%, that it belonged to the Lord. But we just didn't think we could afford it. And really, that was the problem: we were trusting our budget more than we were trusting our God.

Looking back, I realize we were holding tight to our money because we hadn't yet learned to hold tight to God.

But when God got a hold of our hearts, everything changed. We surrendered. We trusted. And when we finally started giving faithfully, even when it felt risky, we learned a life-changing truth: *God always provides for those who trust Him.*

Now I'm not saying tithing makes everything easy. I'm saying it reveals whether you're serious. Whether you believe that everything you have comes from God, and that everything you give is an act of worship, not an act of loss.

So why start this chapter with that kind of story?

Because as a trustee, this topic isn't just about balancing numbers, it's about *living with integrity*. And if God's people are giving in faith, then we'd better be just as faithful in how we steward what they give. This isn't pocket change, it's sacrifice. This isn't bookkeeping, it's spiritual responsibility.

And you can't protect what you're not personally surrendered to.

So, let's talk about financial integrity not as accountants, but as men of God. Men who've learned to trust Him, to lead by example, and to handle the sacred resources of the church in a way that honors both the people who gave and the God they gave it to.

Because every dollar in the offering plate is someone's act of <u>worship</u>. It's sacred. And God expects us to treat it that way.

Honesty Before the Lord and Men

When it comes to finances, it's not enough for the books to balance; the heart has to be right, too. That's why financial integrity starts long before a dollar is spent. It begins with a deep conviction: that everything we do, we do openly before the Lord and visibly before His people.

Paul understood this, which is why in **2 Corinthians 8:20–21,** he wrote:

"Avoiding this, that no man should blame us in this abundance which is administered by us: Providing for honest things, not only in the sight of the Lord, but also in the sight of men."

In other words, Paul wasn't just focused on doing right. He wanted to ensure there was no hint of mishandling. He knew how quickly money could damage ministry if it wasn't handled with care.

And I'll be honest with you, I've seen firsthand how quickly trust can be lost in a church over finances. Not because someone stole money. Not even because something was mishandled. But simply because things weren't clear. When members start asking, *"Where's the money going?"* and nobody answers, or worse, people get defensive, it opens the door for assumptions. And those assumptions turn into whispers. And those whispers start to shape the testimony of the whole church.

At FaithWay, we have a simple standard: **do what's right and ensure it's right.** Don't just say, *"The Lord knows my heart."* That's not enough. The people ought to know your actions. And if we're dealing with God's money, then let's treat it as if we're going to give an account to Him for every dollar, because we will.

Let me provide a real-life example. I remember a time early in the church plant when we had to decide whether to buy a small set of chairs or save that money for rent. It wasn't a big purchase, maybe a few hundred dollars, but I felt it. And I knew if anyone asked, *"Was that wise?"* I needed to be able to answer without squirming.

That's what financial integrity looks like. It's not just knowing what's allowed; it's doing what's right and being ready to explain it with clarity and peace.

And as trustees, you help build that kind of culture. Your role isn't just reviewing reports; it's reinforcing the trust behind those reports. Your questions, your oversight, and your presence at the table all send a message that we take stewardship seriously. It says that we're not hiding anything, that we welcome accountability, and that we're not just trying to be compliant, we're striving to be clean before God and transparent before His people.

You don't need to be a financial expert. You just need to be a man of integrity. Because what takes years to build with a church family can be destroyed in five minutes if money is handled incorrectly or even perceived as such.

So, here's a question I ask myself often: *"Would I be comfortable standing before the entire church and explaining this decision?"* Whether I do or not, God already saw it.

That's the standard, that's the calling, and that's the kind of integrity that protects a ministry, honors the givers, and pleases the Lord.

Trustees Help Safeguard the Process

Let's clear something up right out of the gate: Trustees don't control the money. That's not what this role is about. You're not here to micromanage. You're here to protect. Big difference.

You see, when people hear the phrase *"financial oversight,"* they often picture a committee sitting around a table, voting on how much ink to buy for the printer or whether the pastor can order gospel tracts. That's not oversight, that's overreach. And it's a recipe for frustration, burnout, and spiritual paralysis.

I've been on the other side of this, and I've seen how hard it is for a pastor to lead when he has to get a green light for every little thing. It's exhausting. But I've also seen the beauty of a healthy trustee team, men who aren't trying to tie things down, but who are standing guard to make sure nothing slips through the cracks. That's what this section is about.

You're not the budget enforcer.
You're the budget protector.

So, what does that look like practically? Here's how trustees help safeguard the process in a way that builds trust instead of tension:

- **Counting the Offerings**

    At FaithWay, our trustees assist in counting and recording the offerings after each service. We never have one person count alone. Not because we expect dishonesty, but because we want to remove the appearance of it. It's about accountability. It's about honoring what people gave in faith. When someone gives sacrificially, the last thing we should do is handle that carelessly.

- **Oversight of Major Expenses**

    If a significant expense is approaching, whether it's equipment, a lease agreement, or a contract, we want wisdom in the room. That doesn't mean you make the final call, but it does mean you're watching with me. A second set of eyes is a gift. Ask the questions that need asking, not to stop things, but to ensure nothing is being overlooked. Because we'd rather slow down for a day than backtrack for a year.

- **Monthly Reviews of Church Finances**

    Every month, we review the church's giving, spending, and budget alignment together. It's not a time for nitpicking, it's a time to make sure we're stewarding well. You help confirm that our financial direction supports our spiritual mission. Because we don't want to fund habits, we want to fund harvest.

- **Serving as a Sounding Board**

    Sometimes the pastor or treasurer will hit a crossroads: *"Do we make this investment? Do we wait? What's the right step here?"* That's when you're a gift. Not as a critic. Not as a controller. But as a faithful, wise counselor. Your presence says, *"You're not in this alone. Let's pray through it together."*

Our goal as a leadership team is to build a culture where no one has to wonder if the finances are being handled wisely, because they know they are.

You don't need to have an accounting degree to be a trustee. But you do need a clear heart, a trustworthy spirit, and a willingness to say, *"Let's make sure we're honoring the Lord with every decision."*

You're not there to slow things down. You're there to help the ministry move forward with confidence and integrity.

Avoiding Conflict Through Transparency

If there's one thing that can derail a healthy church faster than anything else, it's *money confusion*. Not misuse. Not a scandal. Just plain old confusion.

Most church conflicts about money don't start because something was done wrong. They start because something wasn't explained well. People aren't usually angry because of what was spent, they're unsettled because no one told them why. And when people don't understand what's going on, they start filling in the blanks themselves. That's where assumptions grow, and assumptions rarely lead to anything good.

I've seen it firsthand. One small decision, such as buying new equipment or renting a new room, can suddenly become the subject of hallway conversations, not because people are against it, but because no one has ever told them about it. That's why transparency isn't just good stewardship, it's **wisdom**.

Here at FaithWay, we've committed to this principle: We don't just want to do the right thing; we want our people to know it's being done right.

And this is where you come in.

As a trustee, you play a crucial role in maintaining open and clear lines of communication. You don't need to know every detail down to the penny. But you should be familiar with the process. Familiar enough to help someone understand how we operate. Familiar enough to give calm, clear answers when someone asks a sincere question.

You're not the church accountant or the final decision-maker. But you are a bridge. A stabilizer. Someone who can say, *"Here's how we do things, and here's why you can trust the process."*

Here are just a few ways that happens:

- **Helping with Reports and Updates**

    When we share financial reports with the church, whether quarterly, annually, or for special projects, you're part of that. When you've seen the numbers, asked your questions, and been part of the conversation, you can stand behind the report with confidence. That builds trust.

- **Being Available to Answer Questions**

    Sometimes people just want clarity. They're not trying to stir up trouble; they just didn't understand something. And a calm, grace-filled explanation from a trustee can go a long way in removing suspicion and building confidence. Remember, most folks aren't looking for control; they're looking for clarity.

- **Encouraging Better Communication**

If you notice that we could have explained something more clearly or sooner, please let us know. Not with frustration, but with wisdom. *"Pastor, maybe next time we can include this in the report..."* or *"That might be something worth mentioning on Sunday."* That's how we grow, not by avoiding feedback, but by learning from it.

Proverbs 11:3 says,

"The integrity of the upright shall guide them: but the perverseness of transgressors shall destroy them."

In other words, **integrity creates stability**. When people know that upright men are helping lead, they stop questioning every move. They stop worrying about hidden motives. They rest easier, knowing things are being handled in the light.

So be that man. Be the calm presence in the room. Be the clear voice in the hallway. Help protect the unity of the church not just by what you do, but by how you communicate it.

Because when integrity leads the way, trust follows closely behind.

Money Is a Tool, Not the Mission

Let me say something plainly: **We are not here to raise money. We're here to reach people!**

If we're not careful, churches can start behaving like businesses. Budgets become barriers. Fear starts calling the shots. And the mission, the actual calling to reach souls, gets buried under spreadsheets and savings goals.

Now don't misunderstand me. I believe in budgeting. I believe in counting the cost. The Bible teaches that. But I've also seen what happens when we let finances become the final word on everything. Suddenly, we stop asking *"Is this what God wants?"* and start asking *"Can we afford it?"*

Let me tell you something that stirs me up: I've seen prosperity preachers stand on stages, manipulating people into giving, all while misusing those funds for luxury and control. That's not ministry. That's **spiritual fraud**. And it has nothing to do with the church Jesus bled and died for.

The true mission of the church is to proclaim the gospel of Jesus Christ. Everything else, including money, is meant to serve that mission.

That's why we must ask ourselves, as trustees: *Are we using God's money to fuel God's mission, or are we hoarding it to protect our comfort?*

We don't give to build bigger bank accounts. We give to build the Kingdom. The money that comes in isn't for us to sit on, it's for us to **steward forward**. That means if God opens a door, we don't close it because it's *"not in the budget."* We don't shrink back from ministry opportunities because we're nervous about the numbers. We pray, we count the cost, and then we **step forward in faith.**

Let me share something personal: there was a time in our ministry when the numbers didn't make sense. Giving was down. Bills were up. And God laid it on our hearts to give generously to another ministry in need. It didn't make sense on paper. But we did it anyway, and can I tell you something? God met every single need we had and more.

You see, when you give by faith, you're not being reckless you're being **obedient**.

Luke 12:34 says,

"For where your treasure is, there will your heart be also."

If all our treasure is sitting in a bank account, maybe it's time to check where our heart is.

The church doesn't exist to preserve money. It exists to **proclaim Jesus**. And when we start holding on to funds more tightly than we hold on to faith, we've lost the plot.

So, here's the challenge:

Don't let the budget become a reason to say *"no"* to God. Let the budget be a tool that helps us say *"yes"* with wisdom.

Because at the end of the day, **God doesn't bless us just so we can feel secure. He blesses us so we can be a blessing.** The question isn't *"How much do we have?"* The question is, *"What does God want us to do next?"*

That's the kind of mindset trustees must have. One that sees every dollar as fuel for the mission and every decision as an opportunity to demonstrate faith.

Let's not play it safe. Let's steward with courage. Let's be the kind of men who trust God more than we trust our calculators.

What We've Learned in This Chapter

This chapter wasn't just about money. It was about **trust**.

We started with a personal question: *Do you give faithfully?* Because before a man can help steward the finances of the church, he must first surrender his own. You can't help guard the trust of others if you haven't proven trustworthy yourself. Giving isn't about income; it's about obedience. It's not a math problem, it's a heart issue.

And until we settle the matter of the tithe in our own lives, we can't be the kind of leaders the church needs.

We also saw that every dollar in the offering plate is more than currency; it's a testimony. It's someone's faith in action. It's the widow's two mites. It's a young couple learning to trust God for the first time. That means the way we handle those funds must reflect the same faith and reverence that went into giving them.

Financial integrity isn't just about keeping clean records. It's about **maintaining a pure heart** before God and others. The Apostle Paul didn't just manage money; he protected the testimony that went with it. And that's what trustees must do too.

You help count the offerings, not just for accuracy, but for accountability. You review the monthly reports not just to spot errors, but to confirm we're still aligned with our mission. You ask the hard questions not to challenge leadership, but to support it with wisdom and clarity.

You're not the watchdog; you're the **gatekeeper of integrity.**

We also learned that most financial conflicts in churches don't come from corruption. They come from confusion. And when things are unclear, people start filling in the blanks. That's why trustees serve as a bridge between leadership and the people, helping explain, clarify, and reinforce the systems that protect the ministry and promote trust.

Finally, we were reminded that money is not the mission, it's just the tool. The church exists to proclaim Christ, not protect the bottom line. So, we don't let fear hold us back from faith. We don't serve the budget; we use the budget to serve God.

So, here's the challenge:

Be faithful. Be generous. Be clear. Be surrendered. And above all, be the kind of man who handles God's money in a way that reflects God's heart.

That's a trustee worth trusting.
That's a steward God can bless.
And that's the kind of leader this church needs you to be.

CHAPTER 7:
TEAMWORK AND UNITY WITH CHURCH LEADERSHIP

A few months into planting FaithWay, I was sitting in my office after a Sunday service, completely exhausted. Not because of the preaching. Not even because of the setup or the takedown. But because I felt like I was carrying the whole thing alone.

Now, don't get me wrong, I love serving, and I'll be the first to admit that some of that pressure was my fault. I was still learning how to delegate, still figuring out who I could lean on. It's hard in those early days to let go of the reins, even when you know you need to.

But it wasn't until one of the men came up to me and said, *"Pastor, you don't need to do it all, let us help,"* that things began to shift. It wasn't just what he said, it was how he said it. He meant it. And over time, others followed.

Today, I smile when I watch one of our men step in and lift something before I even have the chance to reach for it. I've seen our leaders work side by side, without needing a spotlight, just wanting to serve. And I'll be honest, it's one of the sweetest blessings in the ministry.

It communicates to me their care for their pastor, and it shows their love for Christ and their devotion to the church He's building. It tells me they're not just attending, they're abiding. They're not looking for credit, they're looking for ways to lift the load. And that kind of spirit? That doesn't just build trust, it magnifies the grace of God.

It creates a culture where the work of God isn't carried by one man, but by a team of faithful men walking in unity under the leadership of Christ.

So, how are you supporting your pastor? It's not just a practical question, it's a biblical one. Scripture shows us over and over again that when God calls a man to lead, He calls others to walk with him.

Think about **1 Thessalonians 5:12–13:**

"And we beseech you, brethren, to know them which labour among you, and are over you in the Lord, and admonish you; And to esteem them very highly in love

for their work's sake. And be at peace among yourselves."

That's a calling to recognize spiritual leadership and respond not with distance or critique but with love, honor, and peace. It's not about putting a man on a pedestal; it's about understanding the weight he carries and walking in step to support him.

Then there is **Exodus 17,** one of the clearest examples of pastoral support in action. Moses was on the mountain, holding up the rod of God as Israel fought the enemy below. As long as his hands were raised, the battle went in Israel's favor. But when his hands dropped, the tide turned.

He couldn't do it alone, and his strength gave out. And that's when Aaron and Hur stepped in. They didn't take the rod; they held up his arms. One on each side. Quietly, faithfully, and without needing recognition.

That's the role of a trustee. **You're not called to carry the rod. You're called to carry the man who's holding it.**

I've had those moments, more than I can count. Moments when I could feel the weight of the ministry getting heavier. The sermon was ready, the room was full, but I was drained. And then a brother came along and said, *"Pastor, let me take care of that."* And just like that, my arms were lifted, my spirit was strengthened, and I was ready to lead again.

So, let me ask it another way: When your pastor feels the weight of the battle... will he find you standing at his side?

Because support isn't just a sentiment, it's a shared burden. And every time you step in with that mindset, you're not just doing a task, you're building a team. You're showing your pastor he's not carrying the vision alone.

Building Together: Nehemiah's Team

I love **Nehemiah 3**. It's one of those chapters that might seem boring at first glance, a long list of names and assignments, but if you slow down and really take it in, it's powerful. You see families, craftsmen, priests, even goldsmiths and perfume makers, all working side by side to rebuild the walls of Jerusalem.

They weren't all builders by trade, but they were faithful to the task. Each one showed up, took ownership of their section, and gave their best. And because of that shared dedication, what should have taken years was done in just 52 days.

That's the power of unity! It reminds me of all the work God has done through FaithWay. We're still a young church, but we've seen God do amazing things. And I believe one reason for that is simple: our people work together. They don't wait to be asked. They don't shrug off responsibility. They simply see a need and meet it with joy, humility, and a heart.

And can I say something? That's where the real strength of a church is found. Not in the size of the budget or how polished the stage looks, but in the willingness of God's people to take ownership of their section of the wall.

In Nehemiah's day, no one said, *"That's not my job."* They just showed up. They each had different roles and skills, but the same mission: to see God's work move forward.

And here's the thing, not every section was exciting. Some repaired gates. Others rebuilt towers. And I'm sure someone had the not-so-glorious job of clearing rubble. But it all mattered. Because when every part is done faithfully, the whole wall stands strong.

That's the same heart I pray for in our trustees. You may not always get noticed. You may never be thanked from the pulpit. But when you step in and carry your portion with excellence and humility, you're helping protect what God is building. You're strengthening the hands of your pastor. And you're showing others what it looks like to serve with faithfulness.

Nehemiah 3 reminds us that ministry isn't just about what happens in the pulpit, it's about what's being built behind the scenes. And the men who step in, shoulder to shoulder, to serve quietly, consistently, and joyfully, those are the ones who help keep the wall standing.

So don't wait to be asked. Don't look for recognition. Just grab a brick, pick up the tools, own your section and build like it matters, because it does.

The Trustee's Place in the Team

Let me encourage you by telling you that you're not on the outside looking in. You're in this, and you're a part of the team.

As a trustee, you're not a detached observer with a clipboard. You're a part of the body. A brother in the trenches. One of the men God has entrusted to protect and support what He's doing through the local church. That means you're not just a title-holder, you're a team member.

However, let me warn you from experience that churches can quickly get off track when trustees forget this important principle.

I've observed some churches where trustees view themselves more as referees than teammates. They believe their role is to keep score, blow the whistle, and control the pace. But that's not biblical stewardship, that's carnal control. And it doesn't protect the church. Instead, it does just the opposite. It weakens it.

Trustees don't exist to keep the pastor *"in check."* They exist to help carry the weight of ministry under pastoral leadership. You're not at the top of some imaginary chain of command; you're at the base, helping hold things together with humility and strength.

Philippians 1:27 lays it out clearly: *"...stand fast in one spirit, with one mind striving together for the faith of the gospel."*

That's your lane. That's your mindset. Striving together. Not dragging your feet. Not pulling against the leadership. Not waiting to be convinced. But leaning in because you believe in the mission and want to be part of how God moves it forward.

Now let's talk reality.

Sometimes a new trustee comes in eager and ready to serve... and one of the old trustees pulls him aside and says, *"Hey, slow down. You're making the rest of us look bad."*

Brother, if that ever happens to you, let me tell you right now: don't listen to it. That spirit isn't biblical, it's toxic. Don't let someone else's laziness set the pace for your obedience.

You weren't called to protect anyone's ego. You were

called to help build the church. You were trusted with a task. Don't let anyone talk you out of it.

And if you ever catch yourself slipping into that mindset where you're coasting, waiting for someone else to act first, snap out of it. Go back to Nehemiah. Go back to your calling. Go back to your pastor, and ask, *"Where can I help? What can I carry? How can I strengthen what God's building here?"*

That kind of spirit changes everything.

Let's be painfully honest, the church doesn't need another man with opinions. It needs men with ownership. Men who walk in with their sleeves rolled up and their hearts surrendered. Men who aren't looking for power, but for purpose.

Because when trustees walk in unity with their pastor and with one another... when they understand that they're part of the team and not above it... That's when the church moves forward with confidence, with clarity, and with strength.

So, ask yourself this:

- Am I supporting the mission or slowing it down?

- Am I building alongside my pastor or watching him carry the weight alone?

- Am I a team player or a silent observer?

If you've been trusted with the task, then walk like it. Work like it. And serve like someone who's honored to be part of what God is doing.

COMMUNICATION IS KEY

If you've done ministry for more than five minutes, you already know that most problems in church life don't come from what was done wrong. They come from what was said wrong or, worse, from what wasn't said at all.

I've seen churches divided, not over doctrine or scandal, but over silence. One person assumes, another misreads, and before long, what should have been a simple conversation becomes a full-blown argument. And if the devil can't get in through sin, he'll try to sneak in through confusion. That's why communication isn't just helpful, it's spiritual warfare.

As a trustee, you're in a unique position. You have the pastor's trust, and you're close enough to the leadership to understand the heart behind certain decisions. Because of that, you'll hear things that aren't meant for the congregation, such as conversations that are private, confidential, and must be handled with discretion. This is not a role for gossip; it's a call to stewardship.

If you struggle with wanting to *"fill people in"* or *"sound in the know,"* this role will be a spiritual battle for you. Because trustees must walk the fine line between access and arrogance, and awareness without indiscretion.

Proverbs 11:13 says,

"A talebearer revealeth secrets: but he that is of a faithful spirit concealeth the matter."

There are times when someone in the church has a sincere question and needs a little help understanding what's going on. In those moments, you can be a bridge and not a wall. You can provide clarity and answer with grace, without undermining the pastor's leadership. And if you don't know the answer, point them directly to the pastor or church leadership with full confidence.

But there will also be times when someone isn't looking for understanding; they're looking for ammunition. They want details so they can stir up controversy. Or worse, they want you to side with them on something they haven't even discussed with the pastor. And that's when you must lead with maturity.

Here's what that sounds like: *"That's not my place to share, but I'd encourage you to talk directly to the Pastor. He'll help you understand."*

So here's some practical wisdom:
- Don't repeat what was said in a private meeting.

- Don't share what you only partially understand.
- Don't vent frustrations just to *"process"* things out loud.
- Don't pretend you're in charge of explaining decisions that belong to the pastor.

Instead:
- Pray before you speak.
- Speak only what's helpful and honoring.
- And when in doubt, be silent.

Because silence isn't weakness, it's wisdom, and when something does need to be said, say it right.

If you have any concern, please bring it to your pastor directly. If there's confusion, seek clarity in private. And if you see another trustee starting to drift toward gossip or public criticism, lovingly remind them to stay on track. That's part of your role, too.

You don't protect the church by keeping everyone in the loop. You protect it by knowing when to close the loop.

Your communication, both what you say and what you *choose not* to say, is one of the clearest reflections of whether you can be truly trusted with the task.

Don't entertain gossip. Don't fuel division. And don't feel pressured to explain things that are above your role. It's okay, and often best, to say, *"You know what? That's something you should ask the pastor directly."* Because sometimes the most spiritual answer is, *"That's not my place to share."*

At the end of the day, your words carry weight. Use them carefully. Use them biblically. Let's be the kind of men who protect with our silence, build with our speech, and know the difference.

Walking in Agreement

Let's face it, there are going to be times when you and your pastor don't see eye to eye. That doesn't make you a bad trustee, and it doesn't make him a bad pastor. It makes you both human.

But here's the test of maturity: Can you still walk together when you don't fully agree?

Amos 3:3 asks,

"Can two walk together, except they be agreed?"

Now that doesn't mean we all like the same paint color, sing the same songs, or have the same opinion on every detail. What it does mean is that we're moving in the same direction, under the same biblical mission, and following the same God-ordained leadership.

Let me put it this way: agreement doesn't mean you like every idea. It means you believe in the man God called to lead. And because of that, you choose to support the direction with humility, faith, and loyalty.

What matters most is that you've prayerfully decided: *"This is the pastor God has placed over me, and I trust the Lord enough to follow his lead, even when it stretches me."*

That's not blind loyalty. That's biblical faith.

Paul reminded the Corinthian church that we are *"labourers together with God"* **1 Corinthians 3:9**.

Not competitors. Not critics. But co-laborers. That kind of unity doesn't just happen. It's chosen. It's guarded. It's a decision to lay down pride and pick up the shovel.

I've had seasons in ministry when decisions needed to be made that not everyone fully understood at the time. Some of them were heavy. Some came with risks. And I wasn't looking for a committee to analyze the direction. I was praying for a team who would help carry the weight.

Sometimes, the greatest support a trustee can offer is not another opinion. It's a quiet, humble *"I'm with you, Pastor."*

Now, let's also be honest. There may come a time, whether from doctrinal differences, major philosophical shifts, or a conviction of conscience, when you can no longer support the direction of the church. If that ever happens, then for the sake of your soul and the health of the body, step back gracefully.

Not in protest. Not in pride. But in peace.

Because holding a position of influence while quietly opposing the leadership will always lead to division, and that's not just unwise, it's dangerous.

But if you can walk together... if you do believe God is leading this church through your pastor... then walk like it.

- Don't just show up, stand up.
- Don't just agree privately, support publicly.
- Don't just nod in meetings, shoulder the vision with strength.

Ephesians 4:3 says,

"Endeavouring to keep the unity of the Spirit in the bond of peace."

That word *"endeavouring"* means you work at it. You guard it. You fight for it. Unity doesn't stick by default. It has to be held together by deliberate, Spirit-led effort.

So, can your pastor count on you? Can he trust that even if you don't understand everything, you'll still walk with him? That you'll seek clarity without causing confusion? That you'll lean in, not pull away?

What We've Learned in This Chapter

This chapter wasn't just about teamwork. It was about trust, unity, and how we walk together as men entrusted with God's work.

We began with a simple but personal reminder: pastors aren't meant to carry the weight of ministry alone. God never designed His church to rest on one man's shoulders. That's why He raises up others to stand beside him, not to take the spotlight, but to help lift the burden. And when that happens, it becomes one of the sweetest blessings a pastor could ever experience.

We were reminded of Nehemiah 3, where ordinary people took on extraordinary tasks, not because they were skilled builders, but because they were committed. They each took ownership of their section of the wall, and because they worked together in unity, the impossible became reality in just 52 days. That kind of faithfulness still builds walls, and it still builds churches.

Then we explored the role of a trustee on the team. Trustees aren't board members on the outside. They are boots on the ground. Not overseers of the pastor, but protectors of the mission. We clarified that you're not there to control the pace of ministry, but to support the momentum God is giving. And we sounded the alarm that laziness, apathy, or passivity among trustees will eventually weigh down the work of God.

So we asked the hard questions:
- *Are you helping or hesitating?*
- *Are you building or just observing?*
- *Are you part of the wall or part of the weight?*

We also learned that communication is a form of spiritual stewardship. That means knowing when to speak, how to speak, and when to stay silent. Trustees are trusted with sensitive information. That trust must be guarded, not paraded. We don't entertain gossip. We don't fuel suspicion. We don't confuse transparency with noise. And when in doubt, we point people to the pastor not to protect a person, but to preserve the peace and purpose of the church.

Finally, we saw that walking in agreement doesn't mean uniformity. **It means unity.**

It means choosing to trust the direction God has given, even when you don't fully understand the method. It means asking questions with humility, not stirring conflict with opinions. And it means being honest with yourself if you can't walk with the pastor in peace, then for the sake of the church, step out of leadership with grace, not resistance.

Because here's what it all comes down to: If you've been trusted with the task, then be the kind of man your pastor can count on. Be the kind of man your church can lean on. Be the kind of man God can use without hesitation.

When trustees walk in unity with leadership, speak with wisdom, serve with faithfulness, and protect with integrity, the church becomes unshakable.

That's the kind of trustee God blesses.
That's the kind of culture we're building.
And that's the kind of man you're called to be.

CHAPTER 8:
LEGAL AND ETHICAL RESPONSIBILITY

When I first became a trustee, no one handed me a handbook. No one sat me down and said, *"This is what you'll be responsible for."* I remember walking into my first meeting unsure of what was expected. I figured I was there to help by showing up early, staying late, possibly carrying some tables, or locking up after service. My heart was willing, but I honestly had no idea that being a trustee meant helping protect the church legally.

No one explained what nonprofit status was, how lease agreements worked, or why insurance policies mattered. I was in the dark. I didn't even realize that many of the responsibilities I'd soon shoulder had serious legal and financial implications, not just for the church, but for the testimony of Christ.

Looking back now, I can see how much confusion came from that lack of clarity. I wasn't trying to shirk my responsibility. I just didn't know what it was. And that's part of the reason this chapter exists.

If you've ever felt that same uncertainty, you're not alone. Many trustees step into the role thinking it's about being handy or helpful, and yes, it often includes that; however, at its core, the trustee role exists to help the church remain legally protected, ethically sound, and spiritually prepared to carry out its mission without distraction or compromise.

But here's something important: this chapter is not about policies and procedures.

Those things vary from pastor to pastor and church to church, and they should. The specific responsibilities you carry as a trustee will be defined by your local church and under the authority of your pastor. Don't expect this chapter to answer every question for your unique ministry. Instead, let it provide you with a framework, a biblical and ethical understanding of the *why* behind the *what*.

Your pastor is the spiritual overseer of the church. It's his responsibility to give direction and clarity for how the trustee role is applied in your local context. Let him lead, and make it your goal to support that leadership with wisdom, humility, and understanding.

Understanding Your Legal Role

As a trustee, you may not be a lawyer or an accountant, but you still carry legal weight. Whether you're serving in Canada, the United States, or anywhere else in the world, churches are not exempt from the legal systems of their respective countries. They operate in the real world, under real governments, with real paperwork, risks, and responsibilities.

That's where you come in.

Now, depending on the size and structure of your church, many of these tasks may already be handled by the pastor or administrative staff. In smaller churches, the pastor may wear multiple hats and rely more heavily on trustees for assistance. In larger churches, you may find that some of the day-to-day compliance or paperwork is already in motion by those on staff.

But here's the key: trustees are still vital. Even if you're not the one filling out the forms or negotiating contracts, your role in *reviewing, asking questions, and offering insight* is still essential. The pastor may carry the oversight, but you support him with accountability, wisdom, and watchfulness.

You don't need to lead every decision, but your awareness, your willingness to ask the right questions, and your heart to protect the ministry are essential to fulfilling your calling as a steward.

Trustees assist the church in fulfilling its basic legal obligations. That might include:

- Reviewing rental or lease agreements.

- Overseeing compliance with insurance and safety requirements.

- Helping maintain nonprofit or charitable status with local authorities.

- Keeping accurate records when required.

- Asking questions to uncover risks before they become problems.

When I was just starting out, I didn't realize the significance of these matters. I once sat in a meeting about a property agreement and didn't even know what we were agreeing to. I nodded along, but deep down, I felt lost. That's when I realized something important: good intentions aren't enough. You have to understand what you're saying "yes" to. That moment changed how I served. It made me more careful, more prayerful, and more committed to learning the responsibilities I had been entrusted with.

STEWARDSHIP AND TRANSPARENCY

One of the most overlooked responsibilities in the local church is maintaining financial and legal transparency. We often focus on preaching and people, and rightly so, but the behind-the-scenes integrity matters just as much to God. The world is watching, and how we handle our business reflects how seriously we take our witness.

In many countries, particularly in places like Canada and the United States, churches registered as charitable or nonprofit organizations are expected to operate with a high level of transparency. This entails regular reporting, accurate record-keeping, and transparent handling of church finances.

You may not be the one logging every receipt or filing every report, but your role is to help ensure that what's being done is being done right. That includes:

- Reviewing financial statements when asked.

- Asking clarifying questions.

- Confirming that donations are being handled according to policy.

- Ensuring proper insurance, safety procedures, and background checks are in place.

- Knowing when to recommend outside legal or financial advice.

Proverbs 22:1 says:

"A GOOD name is rather to be chosen than great riches, and loving favour rather than silver and gold."

The church's name and reputation are worth more than its balance sheet. When trustees act with transparency, they help protect the church's testimony before its members, its community, and even the government.

Let me also say this: **your role is not to micromanage, but to reinforce integrity**. There is a difference between helpful involvement and untrustworthy oversight. Your pastor needs men who care enough to pay attention but are humble enough to follow. If something doesn't look right, speak up with respect. If everything looks good, give confidence and support. That's the balance we're aiming for.

REAL-WORLD SITUATIONS

Every church is different. Some meet in rented spaces, while others own their own property. Some have dedicated staff for operations, others rely entirely on volunteers. But regardless of church size or setting, trustees are often called upon in key moments not necessarily to *run* the show, but to *reinforce* the mission.

Depending on the situation, your pastor or staff may handle most of the day-to-day decisions. That's okay, and in many churches, that's exactly how it should be. But even then, your insight, availability, and willingness to support still matter. Sometimes you'll be called in to review, confirm, ask a few questions, or give an outside perspective.

Here are some common examples:

- **Lease renewals or property negotiations**: Whether you own the building or rent a space, there are legal and financial details that need attention. Trustees can help ask the right questions or confirm the terms.

- **Insurance Reviews**: From property damage to liability coverage, insurance can be a complex topic. Trustees can help ensure the church is protected and appropriately covered.

- **Equipment purchases or maintenance decisions**: Sometimes, trustees are asked to help assess needs, review bids, or offer guidance on major purchases.

- **Financial and budget discussions**: You might not write the checks, but you can help ask wise questions, spot inconsistencies, or confirm accountability practices.

- **Safety and risk management**: Consider fire codes, emergency exits, and policies for background checks in children's ministries. Trustees help protect people and property.

These responsibilities may shift depending on the season of the church. When a church is small or in the process of planting, trustees may be deeply involved in every decision. As it grows, pastors may carry more of the load with staff support, but they'll still need faithful trustees they can count on for accountability, wisdom, and help.

Just remember: **being trusted with the *"small things"* doesn't mean your role is small**. It means your service has helped your pastor sleep better at night, knowing someone else is watching out for the details that could cause big problems later.

Doing What's Right, Even When It's Hard

Sometimes, serving as a trustee means being willing to have hard conversations or making unpopular decisions. It might mean pausing a purchase until the numbers line up. It might mean double-checking insurance policies, reviewing a lease that doesn't feel right, or even asking a difficult question when something seems off.

This isn't about control, it's about careful stewardship.

I've learned that faithfulness sometimes looks like speaking up... and other times, it looks like slowing down. A faithful trustee knows when to say, *"Pastor, I trust your direction. Let me help you carry it out."* And, when to ask, *"Have we looked at this from every angle?"*

Here are a few moments trustees may face:

- Catching an error in a financial report and choosing to address it with grace and truth.

- Realizing a vendor isn't operating ethically and recommending a change, even if it's inconvenient.

- Upholding a safety policy when others think it's unnecessary.

- Encouraging the pastor to seek outside counsel for legal or financial issues.

These aren't always easy choices. But they're the kind that protect the long-term health of the ministry.

Proverbs 11:3 says, "The integrity of the upright shall guide them: but the *perverseness of transgressors* *shall destroy them."*

Integrity isn't just about reputation, it's about direction. When you follow God's principles, you don't just avoid scandal; you help guide the church into long-term strength.

Don't be afraid to stand for what's right. Just be sure you do it in the right spirit with humility, respect, and the goal of **protecting**, not **pressuring**.

A Warning About Misused Influence

Now, let me offer a pastoral warning: sometimes, trustees fall into the trap of using their role to resist progress rather than protect integrity. I've seen it. A trustee may not like a decision, such as a new ministry effort, a budget change, or even a facility move, so they use their influence to delay, deflect, or derail what the pastor and church are prayerfully pursuing.

Brother, that's not stewardship. That's sabotage.

This role is not a platform for personal preferences. It's not a position to protect *"the way things used to be."* Trustees are not called to slow down the mission but to strengthen it. If something feels off, speak up, but always with humility and a heart for the church's future. If you find yourself resisting every step forward, it might be time to ask, *"Am I protecting the church or holding it back?"*

BEST PRACTICES FOR TRUSTEES IN THE LOCAL CHURCH

Now, before we close this chapter, I would like to take a few moments to address a practical aspect of how trustees are structured within a church.

Every church is different. And while your pastor will ultimately decide how the trustee team is organized and assigned, there are a few best practices that I believe are worth sharing. These aren't rules, but rather principles I've observed that bring strength, clarity, and protection to a local body.

1. THERE SHOULD ALWAYS BE MORE THAN ONE TRUSTEE

No man should ever serve as the only trustee in a church. That's not just unwise, it's dangerous. **Proverbs 11:14** reminds us, *"Where no counsel is, the people fall: but in the multitude of counsellors there is safety."*

Having multiple trustees brings accountability, shared insight, and spiritual safety to the decisions being made. I also recommend that churches appoint **an odd number of trustees** (such as three, five, or seven) to avoid deadlocks when consensus is needed. This helps the church move forward without unnecessary division or delay.

2. TRUSTEES SHOULD BE ASSIGNED BASED ON THEIR STRENGTHS

Sometimes, the pastor may assign specific responsibilities to certain trustees. For example, a man with a background in finance might assist in reviewing budgets or overseeing bookkeeping procedures. A trustee with construction experience may be asked to help with building projects. If that's you, use your gifts, but never run solo.

Always run decisions and updates through your pastor.

He needs to be in the loop, not left wondering. When you're asked to take the lead in an area, you're not taking the reins, you're serving in support. If you're more informed in a specific area, then take the time to walk your pastor through the details and help him lead wisely. That's what biblical teamwork looks like.

3. TRUSTEES SHOULD SERVE WITH TERM LIMITS

Let me be clear, I don't believe trustees should serve indefinitely. Even the most faithful man needs a break. I've seen too many good men burn out or grow passive because they never had a chance to rest or reset. I recommend a **three-year term**, followed by a **mandatory one-year break** before being considered again.

That's not punishment, it's protection. It allows new men to grow and serve. It keeps the church fresh and balanced. And it ensures no one person becomes *"the fixture"* in the ministry. Remember: it's not about the title, it's about the trust.

4. THERE SHOULD BE A PROCESS FOR REMOVAL

It's a difficult topic to discuss, but it's necessary. If a trustee no longer meets the spiritual, relational, or ethical expectations of the role or becomes combative, divisive, or neglectful, there must be a process in place for removal. This should be handled biblically (Matthew 18:15–17; Galatians 6:1), prayerfully, and under pastoral leadership, not in anger or retaliation.

The goal isn't to shame anyone; it's to protect the church and preserve the integrity of the office.

What We've Learned in This Chapter

This chapter wasn't just about rules, it was about responsibility. Being a trustee is more than being helpful, it's about being faithful. It's about protecting the church legally, supporting the ministry ethically, and walking with integrity so the mission of the church can move forward without distraction or compromise.

We began by acknowledging that many trustees step into the role unsure of what's expected. I was one of them. That's why clarity from pastors and readiness to learn from trustees is so vital. Without that clarity, frustration sets in and important details get missed. But with understanding comes confidence, and with confidence comes greater stewardship.

We learned that legal stewardship is not just paperwork, it's a real calling. Trustees are not just helpers, they are safeguards. Whether reviewing contracts or asking tough questions, your presence brings a layer of spiritual and practical protection. You don't need to carry every decision, but you must be willing to stand watch with wisdom and care.

We reaffirmed that the pastor leads the church. Trustees don't override that leadership. Instead, they walk alongside it, offering strength, counsel, and quiet faithfulness behind the scenes. It's not about control, it's about partnership under God's design for the local church.

We also recognized that every church is different. Some are small, others large. Some rent, others own. Some have staff, others rely on volunteers. But regardless of those differences, trustees are essential. The structure may vary, but the calling does not. Your pastor may not ask you to do everything, but he will count on you for wisdom and dependability.

We were reminded that integrity is non-negotiable. From financial transparency to ethical decisions, trustees must choose what is right even when it is inconvenient, uncomfortable, or unpopular. The world is watching, and how we conduct ourselves reflects how seriously we take our testimony.

Finally, we saw that the role of trustee must be structured with care. Term limits, shared responsibility, clear assignments, and the ability to remove someone who is no longer qualified are all part of building a strong, biblically-sound leadership team. These aren't just good ideas, they are protections that keep the church healthy for the long haul.

At the end of the day, this chapter reminded us of one thing. Being a trustee is not about gaining control. It's about guarding what matters most. It's about being a faithful steward of what God has entrusted to you, so the church can grow, flourish, and stay focused on the mission of Christ.

Chapter 9:
Growing Spiritually in the Role

Serving as a trustee is more than a task; <u>it's a calling.</u> And while the responsibilities are mostly practical, the role itself can be deeply spiritual if approached with the right heart.

Just as with any ministry, being a trustee can stretch you, grow you, and mature your walk with the Lord. If you only see it as a job, you'll miss the opportunity. But if you approach it as a spiritual act of service, God will use it to shape your character, strengthen your faith, and deepen your joy in Him.

When I first stepped into the role of a trustee, I thought I was signing up to help the physical or financial needs of the church and to take pressure off the pastor. I didn't realize that God was using that role to do a deeper work in me, *not just through me*.

I came in ready to serve, but I wasn't fully aware of how much I still needed to grow. I thought maturity meant showing up, doing the job, and not causing problems. However, as time passed, I came to realize that genuine spiritual maturity in ministry stems not from the amount of work you do, but from the closeness of your walk with the Lord while doing it.

Now, years later, I'm a pastor. And looking back, I can see how God used my time as a trustee to prepare me, not just in terms of responsibility, but also in character. That season taught me how to listen more carefully, pray more intentionally, carry burdens more humbly, and trust God more deeply.

This chapter is for every man who's wondering whether the work he's doing really matters. I can tell you, it does. But not just because of what it accomplishes on the outside. It matters because of how it transforms you on the inside.

And don't forget who you're really serving.

You might say, *"Pastor Steve, I'm serving my pastor and my church."* And yes, that's part of it. But it's not the full picture.

You are serving the Lord Jesus Christ Himself.

That changes everything. It raises the standard, it deepens the purpose, and it reminds us that even when the work feels unnoticed, He sees it all and He's using it to grow you!

So, where do we begin when it comes to growing spiritually in this role?

We begin by getting our heart in the right place.

Because if we're not careful, we can fall into the trap of doing all the work while neglecting the One we're doing it for. And that's where the story of two sisters, Martha and Mary, comes in. Their story provides a powerful illustration of how service and devotion must go hand in hand...

MARTHA'S HANDS AND MARY'S HEART

One of the most important lessons I've learned, both as a trustee and now as a pastor, is that it's entirely possible to serve faithfully and still miss what matters most.

In Luke 10, we see Martha and Mary. Martha was busy preparing and serving, doing what needed to be done. Mary, on the other hand, sat at Jesus' feet, listening. Martha didn't understand why Jesus would allow Mary to *"do nothing."* But Jesus lovingly corrected her: *"Mary hath chosen that good part."*

He wasn't saying Martha's work didn't matter. He was saying Martha's heart needed to slow down.

That hit home for me in a very real way one Family Day weekend back in 2015. We were hosting a big event at church, which included food, games, setup, and cleanup, among other things. I was running around, doing a little bit of everything: hauling tables, ensuring we had enough napkins, and double-checking the grill. I didn't stop moving. Somewhere in the middle of it all, I looked over and saw a brother from church sitting on a bench, quietly praying with someone.

And I realized, I was so busy serving that I had completely forgotten why we were doing it.

That moment humbled me.

Being a trustee, or a leader of any kind, requires Martha's hands. There's work that must be done. The church doesn't function without men who show up early, stay late, and handle the load. But if you're not careful, you can serve from an empty heart.

God doesn't just want your hands. He wants your heart too.

You'll face seasons where the work is constant, such as reviewing budgets, managing maintenance, and answering questions. But don't let the work replace your worship. Make sure you're still spending time with the Lord in prayer, in Scripture, and in quiet moments of reflection. Don't just fix what's broken. Let God speak to you while you serve.

And don't forget that when Jesus gently corrected Martha, it wasn't a rebuke of her effort. It was a call to refocus her heart.

So, serve with Martha's hands. The church needs that. But never lose Mary's heart. Jesus wants that most.

That balance of doing and becoming isn't easy. But it's necessary. Because the truth is, the strength you bring to the trustee role doesn't come from your skillset alone. It comes from your walk with God. You can only serve well out there when you're staying close to Him in here.

That's why the next part of this chapter matters so much. Let's talk about how to stay spiritually sharp while carrying a practical role.

The Spiritual Disciplines Still Matter

Let's slow down for a moment. You might be thinking, *"I already know this part, Pastor. Read my Bible, say my prayers, be faithful in church..."* And yes, you probably do *know* it. But let me ask, are you living it?

Because in the role of a trustee, it's easy to *drift*. You don't mean to, but somewhere along the way, the doing starts to outweigh the being. You're setting up chairs, reviewing lease agreements, checking the sound system, helping with insurance renewals and somewhere in the middle of all that, you forget that *you* still need to be fed. That *you* still need to be shepherded. That *you* still need to sit at the feet of Jesus.

Let me tell you something that might surprise you: I've seen trustees become spiritually dry while still being outwardly dependable. They showed up, stayed late, and did the work, but inside, their soul was running on empty. I've been there myself.

There was a stretch during my early ministry when everything was busy. People needed help. The church had needs. And I was pushing forward, doing all I could to meet them. But quietly, something in me was starting to fade. My Bible reading got shorter. My prayer life became a checklist. I was giving to others without receiving from the Lord. And though no one else saw it, I was on the edge of burnout, not from the weight of the tasks, but from the lack of spiritual nourishment.

That's why I say again, **spiritual disciplines still matter!**

You cannot serve well if you're not being filled. You cannot lead wisely if you're not being led. You cannot protect the church if your own spiritual walls are crumbling.

Here are a few essential areas to keep strong:

1. Stay in the Word

You may not preach, but you still need to hear from the Lord. God's Word isn't just for pastors. It's for every man who wants to live with conviction and clarity. Make time for it daily. Don't just skim, soak. Read slowly. Listen deeply. Ask God to speak to your heart before you try to speak into any situation.

2. Build a Real Prayer Life

You're a protector, a supporter, and an intercessor. That means your prayers are not optional. They're essential. Don't let them become mechanical. Talk to God like He's right there with you, because He is. Pray for your pastor by name. Pray for your church with a burden. Pray for your own heart to stay soft, humble, and usable.

3. Guard Your Spirit

Bitterness, pride, and spiritual fatigue will always try to sneak in. You might not see it coming at first. Maybe someone makes a comment that stings. Maybe a decision doesn't go your way. Maybe you start to feel overlooked. And if you're not careful, those seeds grow roots.

Trustee, don't let the enemy get a foothold in your spirit. You are too important to this ministry to carry unresolved frustration. Keep short accounts with God. Deal with things quickly. Be willing to forgive. Be willing to repent. Protect your spirit as fiercely as you protect the building, because it's even more valuable.

4. Stay Faithful in Church Attendance

This should go without saying, but I've seen it happen too many times not to mention it. A trustee who isn't consistently in the services cannot consistently lead well. You need the preaching. You need the worship. You need to be under the Word just like everyone else.

I say this with love, don't be so busy with church work that you miss church. Be in your place. Be engaged. Let God speak to you, not just through you.

5. Stay Accountable

You don't have to carry every weight alone. If you're struggling, consider speaking with your pastor. If you feel dry, discouraged, or even tempted, speak up. Isolation is a breeding ground for the enemy. Accountability is one of the greatest protections God has given us.

And let me tell you something, I've seen in godly trustees when they walk close to the Lord, it shows. There's a quiet strength, a steady hand, and a peace that doesn't come from a policy; it comes from Jesus.

But even when you're walking closely with the Lord, reading your Bible, staying faithful in prayer, and guarding your spirit, you will still face pressure.

And that's not a sign of failure. It's a sign that you're growing.

You see, serving as a trustee isn't always clean and easy. Sometimes it's messy. Sometimes it's hard. Sometimes the weight of what you're carrying feels heavier than what people realize.

But those pressures? They aren't just obstacles. They're opportunities for God to stretch your faith, deepen your maturity, and teach you how to depend on Him in ways you never have before.

Growth Comes Through Pressure

I wish I could tell you that being a trustee always feels rewarding. That everyone will always thank you, everything will go smoothly, and every decision will be celebrated. But you've probably already figured this out, it doesn't always work like that.

Sometimes, you'll carry burdens no one else sees. You'll feel tension in meetings. You'll face difficult decisions where there isn't a clear right answer. You may even feel torn between people you love and respect who disagree on what should be done.

I've been there.

I recall a particularly challenging season during my tenure as a trustee, when our church was facing a difficult facility issue. We had to make some hard decisions about repairs, finances, and next steps. People had opinions, strong ones. The pastor was carrying the spiritual weight. The people were carrying emotions. And I felt stuck in the middle.

That season taught me how to pray more honestly, listen more deeply, and speak more carefully. It taught me that pressure doesn't mean you're doing something wrong. It means God is at work within you.

James 1:2–4 says:

"My brethren, count it all joy when ye fall into divers temptations; Knowing this, that the trying of your faith worketh patience. But let patience have her perfect work, that ye may be perfect and entire, wanting nothing."

Pressure is part of the process.

It's what grows your character. It's what reveals where your trust really lies. It's where God teaches you to stay calm when tensions rise, to wait when you want to act, and to trust when you don't fully understand.

Maybe you're in a season like that now. Maybe things are heavy. Perhaps you feel that your input isn't being heard or that your efforts aren't being appreciated. Maybe you're walking through conflict and wondering if you're even cut out for this.

Let me reassure you: you are. Not because you're perfect. But because God is working in you.

Don't waste the pressure. Let it shape you. Let it push you to the Lord. Let it turn your service into surrender and your role into a place of spiritual growth.

Let God Use You While He Works In You

When I was younger in ministry, I used to pray, *"Lord, use me."* And I meant it. But over time, I learned that God isn't just interested in using me. He's also interested in shaping me. And sometimes, the shaping is the greater work.

As a trustee, you stand in a unique position. You are trusted. You're invited into conversations that many in the church never hear. You carry responsibility that few ever see. But in that space, God is doing more than just using your hands. He's refining your heart.

Think about it: You're being asked to carry weight, stay faithful, solve problems, handle pressure, and support leadership, all without applause. That's not just service. That's sanctification.

God often chooses the unseen roles to do the deepest work.

This role will teach you to be patient.

- It will teach you to listen more and talk less.

- It will teach you to keep showing up when it's inconvenient.

- It will show you how to follow well so that one day, if God calls you to lead, you'll do it with humility.

Every spreadsheet, every late-night call, every moment you carry the burden with your pastor. God sees it, and He's not just keeping a record. He's using it to shape a faithful man.

Philippians 1:6 says:

"Being confident of this very thing, that he which hath begun a good work in you will perform it until the day of Jesus Christ."

God isn't finished with you. This role is part of your preparation. And if you lean into what He's doing not just around you, but *in* you, you'll find that your greatest growth won't come from what you do, but from what He does through you.

What We've Learned in This Chapter

This chapter wasn't just about serving. It was about growing. The trustee role may look practical on the surface, but beneath the tasks and responsibilities lies a deeper opportunity. It is an opportunity to be shaped by God into a stronger, wiser, and more faithful man.

We learned that ministry maturity doesn't come from simply showing up or completing assignments. It comes from walking closely with the Lord while you serve. It comes from having Martha's hands without losing Mary's heart.

We saw how spiritual disciplines are not optional for leaders. **They are essential!** A trustee who stays in the Word, builds a genuine prayer life, guards his spirit, remains faithful in church, and remains accountable will serve with more than competence. He will serve with power.

We discovered that pressure is not our enemy. It is part of how God grows us. The burdens we carry, the unseen sacrifices, and the moments of tension are not wasted. They are tools in the hands of a God who is shaping us from the inside out.

And we were reminded that God doesn't just want to use us. He wants to change us. Every meeting, every decision, every late-night text or early morning setup is part of a process where He is making us more like Christ.

So don't miss it. Don't just carry the load. Let it carry you closer to Him. Because being a trustee is not only about what you do for the church. It is about who you are becoming for the Lord.

Chapter 10: Faithfulness in the Background

I still remember one of the first times I served as a trustee and had to come in early to unlock the building. It was cold, the lights were slow to come on, and there was no one else around. I walked through the empty hallway, flipping switches, making sure everything was ready, but I also wondered if it really mattered. Would anyone notice if I hadn't come? Would anyone care?

Now, years later, as a pastor, I can tell you with absolute certainty: **it mattered.**

What I didn't see then was how much peace it gave my pastor knowing he didn't have to worry about those things. I didn't realize that what I thought was *"small"* service was actually part of something sacred, helping God's people gather to hear His Word without distraction.

This chapter is for the man who serves without applause.

The one who unlocks the doors, signs the papers, fixes what's broken, and does what's needed, without needing to be seen.

Your ministry may be in the background, but your faithfulness is not forgotten.

God sees, God knows, and God will reward what no one else notices.

The Value of Hidden Service

Not long ago, I was talking with a man in our church who had just stepped down from a behind-the-scenes ministry role. He said, *"Pastor, I just don't think anyone noticed what I was doing."* And I told him, *"You're probably right, but God did."*

That's what makes your service as a trustee so valuable. It's not just what you do, it's who you're doing it for.

Jesus said in **Matthew 6:4:**

"...and thy Father which seeth in secret himself shall reward thee openly."

That's a promise from the mouth of Christ Himself. God sees the secret things. The thankless tasks. The late-night texts. The early mornings and quiet sacrifices. And not only does He see them, He counts them as service to Him.

You may never preach a sermon. Your name might not be on a plaque. But God keeps record of the faithful.

Let's be honest, some ministries are loud. Visible. Celebrated. But the kind of service trustees often provide? It's quiet. It's steady. It's the kind of work that often goes unnoticed... until it's not done.

That's why your faithfulness matters so much.

You're not just keeping things running... You're keeping things healthy. You're not just protecting property... You're protecting peace. And in a world where so many want attention, your quiet consistency reflects the humility of Christ Himself.

"And whosoever of you will be the chiefest, shall be servant of all." **Mark 10:44**

That's the value of hidden service: it's not lesser, it's often greater. Because it's not about being seen. It's about being faithful.

Why Faithfulness Matters

It's easy to assume that effectiveness in ministry is tied to visibility. That the loudest voice, the most recognized name, or the most talented leader is the one God uses most. But the longer I've served the Lord, first as a trustee, now as a pastor, the more I've come to realize that it's not the visible work that keeps a ministry standing, it's the invisible faithfulness behind the scenes.

Some of the most impactful people in the church are those whose names are never called from the pulpit. They don't preach sermons or lead worship. They're not in the spotlight. But they're pillars. And if they stopped doing what they're doing, the church would feel it immediately.

Faithfulness matters because it's what God is looking for. He is not looking for flashiness, popularity, or performance. He's looking for <u>Faithfulness!</u>

1 Corinthians 4:2 *says,*

"Moreover it is required in stewards, that a man be found faithful."

That verse has become a source of comfort and an anchor for me. Faithfulness matters because someone needs to unlock the building before anyone else arrives. Faithfulness matters because someone needs to check the locks, the lights, and the insurance coverage.

Faithfulness matters because when problems come, and they always do, someone needs to be steady enough not to panic, wise enough to pray, and committed enough to stay.

If you're reading this and thinking, *"That doesn't sound very glamorous,"* you're right! It's not. But neither was carrying water for a traveling preacher. Neither was setting up chairs for the early church. Neither was building an ark in the middle of dry land. And yet, every one of those acts of obedience helped change the course of history.

Let me tell you from experience that it's not the one big moment that shapes a church. It's the repeated acts of unseen faithfulness that do. The decisions made on tired nights, the sacrifices made when no one's watching, and the burdens carried without needing recognition.

You may not always get credit here. But God sees, and your pastor feels it, even if he doesn't always say it. And your church is stronger because of it.

Faithfulness doesn't need a microphone. It just needs a man who refuses to quit.

So, stay with it, keep showing up, and keep doing what you know is right. Even when it's thankless. Even when it's hard. Even when it feels like no one notices.

Because God does. And one day, you'll hear the words we're all living for: *"Well done, thou good and faithful servant..."* **Matthew 25:21**

You're Helping Build the Kingdom

At its core, everything we do in the local church should point to the gospel of Jesus Christ. That includes preaching, singing, teaching, and yes, even trustee meetings.

As a missionary church planter, I've come to believe that the role of a trustee is a kind of missionary calling, just with a different kind of passport and a different kind of platform.

Now, I know what you're thinking: *"Here he goes again with the behind-the-scenes talk."* And yes, I've said it often. But this time, I want you to see it through a different lens. Because while trustees may not be the ones traveling across borders or standing behind pulpits, they are still on mission.

Consider this: missionaries prepare the fields, raise support, and endure personal sacrifice so that the gospel can spread unhindered. Trustees do the same, only in a different field. You prepare the church so it can be a sending station. You help guard its testimony, structure its operations, and make sure nothing gets in the way of the gospel being preached freely and clearly.

You may not preach the sermon, but you make sure the lights are on, the rent is paid, and the insurance is current. You may not counsel the broken-hearted, but you help ensure there's a safe, stable place for them to come and find healing. You may not be teaching the children, but you've helped create the structure that makes that classroom possible.

In that sense, your calling is no less spiritual. You're doing what missionaries do. You're preparing the ground so the seed of the gospel can take root and bear fruit.

1 Corinthians 14:40 says,

"Let all things be done decently and in order."

That verse is often applied to worship services, but it's bigger than that. It's a reminder that order creates opportunity. When the church is healthy and stable, the gospel moves forward without hindrance. And you, as a trustee, are part of that order.

You are a missionary of the local church. Not with a pulpit or a passport, but with a purpose. A purpose to make ready a people and a place for the gospel to be heard.

THE FINAL EVALUATION

One day, every one of us will stand before the Lord and give an account, not just for what we did, but for how we did it... and why.

We won't be graded on the number of hours we put in, the number of meetings we attend, or the number of problems we solve. The question won't be, *"Did people see your work?"* It will be, *"Were you faithful with what I gave you?"*

As a pastor, and as someone who once served as a trustee, I think about that often. Because when it's all said and done, I don't want applause, recognition, or even understanding. I want to hear one thing from the Lord who called me:

"Well done, thou good and faithful servant... enter thou into the joy of thy lord." **Matthew 25:21**

That's the moment we're living for. You see, faithfulness is the true measure of spiritual success. Not giftedness. Not position. Not popularity. But quiet, consistent, wholehearted obedience to the task God has placed in front of you.

And for the trustee, that means:

- Being trustworthy when no one is watching.

- Protecting what matters, even when it's uncomfortable.

- Supporting your pastor, even when it's difficult.

- Keeping the mission at the center, even when the maintenance wears you out.

So, stay the course. You're not just preparing rooms or reviewing reports. You're preparing a church for the work of the gospel. You're not just protecting a building, you're protecting a beacon of truth.

And one day, you will stand before the Lord, not as a background helper, but as a servant He trusted with something eternal. So, let's live for that day.

Conclusion: Trusted With The Task

You made it! ***Congratulations!*** You've walked through every page, every principle, every purpose laid out in this book, to not just to learn about the role of a trustee, but to embrace the calling behind it. And now, standing on the other side, I want you to hear this loud and clear:

Well done.

This wasn't just a training. It was a preparation.
- Not just for tasks, but for trust.
- Not just for service, but for stewardship.
- Not just for knowledge, but for Kingdom work.

God doesn't call perfect men. He calls the faithful ones. And if He has called you to this role, He has also promised to equip you for it.

So, stand tall. Not in pride, but in purpose.
- You are a man God can trust.
- You are a servant the church can lean on.
- You are part of the mission that changes lives.

And don't keep this to yourself. If this book has helped you, **share it!** There are others who feel just as unsure as you once did. There are pastors praying for faithful men. There are churches in need of godly trustees. Perhaps someone you know is wrestling with this calling right now. Please pass this on. Let it become part of their journey too.

Keep going. Keep growing.
Keep guarding the church you love.

And when the day comes to lay down the tools and hand over the responsibility, may it be said of you: *"He was a faithful man. Trusted with the task... and true to the end."*

About the Author
Pastor Steven Pratt, Jr.

Pastor Steven Pratt, Jr. is a missionary church planter and the founding pastor of *FaithWay Bible Baptist Church* in Calgary, Alberta.

Sent out with a burden to reach Canada with the gospel and establish strong, Bible-believing churches, he and his family launched FaithWay from a small gathering in their garage. Today, it has grown into a thriving, multi-ethnic congregation reaching communities across southern Calgary.

He is also the founder of **CanadaChurchPlanting.com**, a ministry dedicated to equipping and encouraging missionaries, church planters, and local churches across Canada.

Pastor Steven's preaching and writing reflect his passion for expository teaching, local church health, and training faithful men for ministry. With a heart for practical discipleship, He emphasizes servant leadership, spiritual integrity, and the kind of stewardship that strengthens both pastors and the churches they serve.

Pastor Steven, his wife Laura, and their daughter Elizabeth are missionaries sent out of *Bible Baptist Church* in Wilmington, Ohio. Together, they count it a privilege to serve the Lord in full-time ministry.

www.ingramcontent.com/pod-product-compliance
Lightning Source LLC
Chambersburg PA
CBHW032229080426
42735CB00008B/775